ENDURING CHILDHOOD ABUSE

ENDURING CHILDHOOD ABUSE

A True Story of a Brave Little Girl Surviving With God's Grace

Connie France Webster

Copyright © 2020 by Connie France Webster

All rights reserved. No part of this book may be used or reproduced in any manner, whatsoever, except in the case of reprints in the context of reviews, without written permission.

Paperback ISBN: 978-17357435-0-9
Hardback ISBN: 978-17357435-1-6

Editor: Amy Pattee Colvin
Cover Design: 100covers.com
Interior Design: Amy Pattee Colvin

CONTENTS

Chapter 1: DANGER AT HOME	1
Chapter 2: KIDNAPPED	11
Chapter 3: LEAVING CHICAGO	16
Chapter 4: THE 911 CALL	23
Chapter 5: BROTHER BETRAYAL	37
Chapter 6: THE LOST CHILD	48
Chapter 7: MOVING OUT	63
Chapter 8: SAVED BY GOD'S ANGEL	73
Chapter 9: NEW CITY	79
Chapter 10: FIGHTING TEMPTATION	87
Chapter 11: BLESSING THE HOUSE	99
Chapter 12: AN UNEXPECTED SURPRISE	105
Chapter 13: FINALLY, I'M FREE	108

ACKNOWLEDGMENTS

I'd like to start out by thanking my wonderful young son, Elijah, for believing in me and giving me total support while I wrote this book, even when things were exceedingly difficult for the two of us.

I'd also like to thank my beautiful editor Amy Pattee Colvin, for being the amazing person she is to see my vision for my book.

I'd like to thank my wonderful grandparents, Arnary and LeRoy, for their bravery, and for stepping up when they sensed something was wrong. If they hadn't, I wouldn't be here today to write this book, and of course, let's not leave out my aunts and uncles for helping when they needed to.

Also, let us not forget to thank everyone on my publishing team. The world is a better place, thanks to people who want to develop and lead others, and who share the gift of their time to mentor future leaders.

Thank you to everyone who strives to grow and help others grow. Without the experiences and support from my peers and team at Love Authentic Living Team, Self Publishing School, **Gary Williams—my very own Yoda**—Natalie Ledwell, and Lisa Nichlos, this book would not exist. You have given me the opportunity to lead a great group of individuals—to be a leader of great leaders is a blessed place to be.

Thank you.

1: DANGER AT HOME

Girl, I want to tell you about my early years. I haven't spoken of this much, but I knew you'd hear me out. It feels good to get this out of my mind and heart, knowing I'm surrounded by your warm embrace.

I was about four years old when my mom married my stepdad. We lived on the Southside of Chicago; Mom was still a party girl, and when she went out, she left us with our stepdad. He waited until he knew she was gone, and then he began beating on us and making us do sexual things to him.

When mom finally got home, I went to her while she was in the bathroom, and I told her how our stepdad beat us and made us put our hands in his pants to touch his wiener, which we did not want to do.

After hearing this, she asked, "What kind of things did he make you do?"

"He puts my hand on his private parts in his pants whenever you leave us with him."

"Honey, I will talk to him about that because he shouldn't be making you do anything like that to him."

Mom found our stepdad and said, "Fat, what are you beating the kids for? And why are you having them touch you, inappropriately?"

"Because when I ask them to do something, they don't listen to me. If I'm the man of this house, then they need to know that I am. As far as me having them touch me, it's not true. Which one of them told you this?"

Girl, everything he said to my mom was a lie, and I believe she fell for it because she was afraid of him.

That night I heard the two of them arguing, and a few minutes later, after a couple of loud banging sounds in their bedroom, I heard her crying. Most of the walls were very thin. We couldn't see through them, but we could hear everything that went on. Our bedroom was right next to their bedroom, and whenever they fought, we heard them.

The next day mom had a red mark around her right eye, so she just stopped asking me anything about what happened in the house whenever she left during the weekday. Our stepdad continued abusing us.

He came into our bedroom and told us, "I know it was one of you kids who told your mom that I was beating you and making you do things that you didn't want to do. I want to know which one of you told her. So come clean, or all of you will be beaten."

We were all so scared of him. I didn't want my siblings to get in trouble, so I said, "It was me."

He then told me to go to his room and wait for him there; I was so scared that I wet myself. He walked in and told me to bend over on the bed. I did what he told me, and he began beating me. He beat me so bad the belt became covered in blood.

When mom came home, she started cooking dinner, and she noticed that I wasn't in the dining room with the other kids. She came into my bedroom, and she saw me lying on the bed. She asked, "Honey, why isn't you in there playing with the other kids?"

"I don't feel good; can I stay in my room?"

She walked over to the bed, sat beside me, and pulled my pants down, exposing the bloody bruises on my butt. She said to me, "Baby, I'm sorry that he did this to you, but Sweetie, you have to do whatever he tells you to do so he won't beat you like this anymore. If he needs you to put up your toys or your clothes, please do what he says, okay?"

I started crying, and I nodded my head, saying, "Yes, I will."

That Friday evening, my sister Edwina and I played a game on the couch in the dining room. We rocked back-and-forth, enjoying ourselves. It was after dinner, which was about two hours before bedtime, and as soon as we started our game, we heard our stepdad yelling from the living room, "You damn kids knock it off back there!"

After he yelled at us from the living room, we looked at each other as though we weren't doing anything wrong. It didn't make sense to us because the couch wasn't making any squeaking sound.

I believe it was the sound of joy coming from two very happy children playing together that he couldn't handle, which meant putting fear in us. The way those old buildings were built, the living room had a long hallway that led to the kitchen and dining room, which meant he was really trying to listen in on us kids and could hear us playing.

The two of us looked at each other again with our hands over our mouths, trying not to laugh out loud. Within a second, our stepdad came into the dining room and began beating on my sister with his belt. While he beat her, I ran to the living where mom was and jumped on her lap, saying, "We weren't doing anything wrong, Mom, just playing a game with each other!"

Then I heard him come into the living room. At that moment, I held onto mom tightly, but his grip was strong, and he started pulling me away from her.

He said to Mom, "Ruby let her go now! You and I have discussed this already. These kids need to learn some discipline around here; they need to know who's the man of the house and the only way that will happen if I take control around here. You heard me when I yelled back there, telling them to stop making so much noise. They just continue as if I said nothing to them; are you telling me, Ruby, that you didn't hear them?"

Mom said, "Fat, I didn't hear them until you turn the TV down. If you wouldn't have turned the TV down, I don't believe you would have heard them back there playing either. All they were doing is having some fun before bedtime. Why can't you just let them be kids? Don't you see where we live, Fat? It is not like they can go outside and play without being attacked by other older kids, or maybe even worse things could happen living here on the Southside of Chicago. They are better off being inside where we know that they will be safe, and I don't see anything wrong with them playing together on the couch."

He looked at my mom with evil in his eyes, and said, "If you don't teach them how to respect the things you spend your hard earn money on, how will they learn? And if we allow them to play on the furniture, then what does that say about us as parents? They will think it's okay."

That's when he grabbed me from my mom's lap and threw me down the hallway. I hit the triangle-shaped corner of the walls, and as I was falling, I heard my arm crack.

My mom came running back to see what happened. She saw me lying on the floor, then yelled, "Fat, what the hell is wrong with you? Why can't you see that you are way too rough on my kids? You've hurt my daughter too many times." She started crying and began mumbling the words, "Oh my God, something is really not right with her. Why would you throw my daughter down the hallway when she is just a child? You need some help, Fat, and if you don't get help soon, I will leave you because you've gone way too far this time. Are you crazy? We have to take her to the hospital right now."

Girl, apparently, the fall knocked the wind out of me, and when we got to the hospital, the nurse asked mom how I broke my arm.

It was my stepdad who answered her by saying, "She fell down the stairs while playing with her sister."

As the nurse continued asking questions, my mom was still in a panicked state of mind, and I saw the nurse watching both of their faces as the two of them struggled to answer her questions. Clearly, the nurse didn't believe what they were telling her, and at that moment, she admitted me to the hospital.

I settled into the hospital room, and about thirty minutes later, the social worker walked in, asking to speak with my mom alone. At that moment, I saw the look on my stepdad's face; I couldn't believe my eyes. For the first time, I saw the look of fear on his face.

When the social worker asked to talk with mom without him being in the room, and when he stepped out of the room, I was hoping and wishing that my mom would tell her what really happened to me, but mom held back from the social worker. So, the social worker scheduled an appointment with mom to speak with the head social worker on Monday morning.

Meanwhile, I got to stay in the hospital for the weekend, and that's when I met this girl about my age named Lucy; she was Caucasian, and I was African American. The two of us had so much fun over the weekend; I never had so much fun in my life until I met her!

Lucy was at the hospital to have her tonsils removed, and she had an idea to play a trick on the nurses. She thought it would be cool to pretend to be me and see if she could pull it off. Now I thought it was funny because clearly, my skin was darker than hers, and for some reason after the nurses switched shift, they didn't pay attention, which meant we both got to have lots of ice cream over the weekend after dinner.

I noticed that everyone at the hospital was genuinely nice to me, including Lucy and her parents. I do believe that God was showing me that not everyone is evil or hateful towards black people. As a little girl, I felt God was trying to speak to me through the spirit by whispering in my ear, "As you work with the angels, you will start to see how magnificently interconnected the world truly is. Our physical world and spiritual world are all centered upon one thing—love!" We all are a part of him, and we are made of energy. We are beings of God.

At the hospital, I noticed that the majority of the nurses were Caucasian. Girl, my point is I was not treated any differently than Lucy while I was there at the hospital. Everyone was nice and kind to me; as a child, I was not ready for it to end.

Well, the weekend was coming to an end, and Lucy and I had so much fun together during the day. We began to quiet ourselves down for the night, and I could tell she wanted to ask me something. Eventually, she asked, "What happened to your arm?"

"My stepdad broke it."

"How did he do that?"

"I was playing with my younger sister, and he got really angry at us for having fun. What made me so mad was my sister, and I wasn't even making any noise. The two of us were playing on the couch, we just wanted to see who could go the fastest by moving back-n-forth on the couch, and the next thing I heard was him yelling at us. And, get this, he was all the way in the living room where he was watching TV with my mom. Within fifteen minutes after he yelled at us, I saw him standing over us with his belt in his hands as he began beating the two of us."

Lucy said, "Your stepdad beat you and your sister for playing on your couch? My father would never do anything like that to his children. What your stepdad did to you and your sister was wrong. Well, maybe if I ask my parents to adopt you, we could have fun all the time. Would you like to be my foster sister?"

"Yeah, that would be nice, but I don't think my mom would let that happen, even though I would love to be your foster sister. I am happy that you want me to be your foster sister Lucy; I never met or had anyone be as nice to me as you are, or let's just say maybe not since my family moved here to Chicago. I hate the school that I go to. Everyone there is so mean to me and my sisters."

Being a child growing up in a world of hate and violence is every parent's nightmare. According to Mark 12:31, NIV: "You shall love your neighbor as yourself; there is no other commandment greater than these." This is what God wants for all of us, but let us face it, not everyone follows the Bible as they should.

Meeting someone like Lucy was an eye-opener for me. I said to her, "I'm going to ask my mom if I can go and stay with my real dad, and I hope she says yes."

That morning was Monday, and Mom met with the social worker. She didn't say anything to me about her meeting, but when I asked her if I could go and stay with my dad; she told me, "Let me think about it, Sweetie, because I need to talk with him since he and I haven't spoken in a while, okay?"

"Okay, Mommy."

That's when Lucy said to me, "I wish she says yes so you can go live with your father because I don't want you to get hurt by your stepdad anymore. You are my best friend now, and I will be very sad if anything happens to you."

"You are my best friend too, Lucy, and being able to stay with my real dad would mean I don't have to live with my evil stepfather anymore."

Then my mom walked back into the hospital room and said, "Honey, me and your stepdad wants you to get better, and I know that you don't like Fat, especially after what he's done to you, but he is really sorry about it. And, I'm afraid, Sweetie, if you don't tell the social worker that it was an accident, they will take you away from me. So, Sweetie, do you understand what I just explain to you?"

"No, I don't understand, Mommy. Why are you asking me to tell a lie for him? I don't want to go back home because he hates us kids, plus when you leave us with him, he beats us and makes us do things with him, and I don't like it. I want to go live with my daddy. You told me that you would think about it once you talk with him; did you call daddy yet?"

She says to me, "Honey, look, I know that I told you that I would think about it, but the thing is, I don't think your daddy is ready to have a child full time because he just got back from the Army. And at the moment, he is staying with his mother, so it's going to take some time before he is ready to have you come and stay with him, sweetheart. I wanted to tell you, but not until I had spoken to him first."

"Mommy, if you haven't talked to Daddy, how do you know if I can't stay with him and grandma?"

She replied, "Yes, you're right, Sweetie, but I called, and his mother answered. She told me that he wasn't there, so I left a message with her to have him call me when he gets home. But Honey, right now, the social workers will be here in a few minutes to speak with you before we check you out of the hospital. All Mommy is asking from you right now is just to say that you and your sister were playing, and you fell backward then down the stairs. Will you do that for me? And, I promise I won't let him hurt you again."

Now, Girl, at the age of five, I had developed this sense of not believing in adults, and when my mom asked me to do this for her, I knew that it was for my stepdad. Then I suddenly got a knot in the pit of my stomach and said, "Mommy, Grandma told me never to tell a lie, or I'd burn in hell if I did; and that God would be very unhappy with me."

"Honey, everybody tells lies when they need to, especially if it means keeping these white folks from taking your children away from you. This is one of those times when I need you to tell this social worker that you fell down the stairs. Will you please do this for your mommy, Honey?"

She really needed me to tell this lie to keep my stepdad from going to jail or getting in trouble with the department of children and family services. Mom then said to me, "If you tell this one little lie for me, I will let you stay with your grandparents. Will that make you happy, Sweetie?"

Not only was this wrong, but my own mother was teaching me how to lie to adults who were in a position to help us. When the social worker came into my hospital room, she walked over to me, where I sat on the bed. She pulled the chair closer to me, and she sat down then asked Mom, "Mrs. McCloud, I would like it if you would step out of the room for a minute while I speak with your daughter. I only have a few questions that I need to ask her."

When mom walked out and closed the door behind her, the social worker said, "Sweetheart, I know from the statement that my assistant wrote down what your mother and stepdad told her, but I want to hear your side. Is it true that you were playing with your younger sister and you fell down the stairs by accident? Now I want you to know that I'm here to help keep bad people from hurting little children like yourself, and the only way I can do that is for you to tell me your side of what happened. Can you do that for me?"

At that very moment, I could hear my mom's voice playing in my head, so I said, "Yes, ma'am. I was playing with my sister, and I fell down the stairs. My mom came to see what happened, and that's when she saw me laying there at the bottom of the stairs."

She responded, "And you're telling me that you were playing with your sister, and that's when you lost your balance, is that right?"

"Yes, ma'am."

"Okay, Sweetheart, thanks for speaking with me. I bet you are ready to get out of this place and go home to your sisters and brothers."

"Yes, ma'am."

She sighed, "Alright, then I'm going to speak with your mother and see about getting you checked out of here. How's that?" As I shook my head to her question, she got up from the chair and walked toward the door, and I saw her talking to my mom.

Girl, it was so hard for me to keep from looking sad when this lady asked me that last question. The truth was I didn't care about going back to our house as long as my stepdad was living there. All I was thinking about was going to live at my grandparent's house.

As Mom stood outside my hospital room, I started to feel guilty about lying to the social worker. Even though my mom asked me to tell the lie, it was the Holy Spirit who placed the guilt on my heart, and, according to Proverbs 12:22 ESV: "Lying lips are an abomination to the Lord, but those who act faithfully are his delight." Even though my mother asks me to lie, it was meant to keep us from going into the system. Surely that was an act of good faith in God's eyes.

Mom came back into the room, and shortly after the social worker passed the nurse's station, my stepdad walked in right behind Mom with a stuffed rabbit. As if that stuffed animal would make me forget about what he had done to me. He handed it to me and said, "Hi, Rabbit, I thought you would like this since you are our little rabbit; everyone misses you at the house, and they can't wait to see you."

When I got home from the hospital, things were not any different. Sometimes I asked Mom, "When am I going to Daddy and Grandma's house?"

"As soon as I get a hold of him, Sweetie." It was like she was trying to brush me off. Eventually, I realized she never spoke with my Dad, so I stopped asking.

2: KIDNAPPED

Now that next weekend came, and Mom was sleeping, and my stepdad was still being abusive toward me and my siblings. He came into my bedroom and told me to go with him. As I got out of my bed, he took me to the study next to the living room and started putting his hand under my pajamas.

He began touching me in the place where no one should be touching a child, and when he finished, he told me not to tell my mom because she wouldn't understand the special bond between a dad and his daughter. He said it was okay, and it was important to keep this between us. Then he said in an evil voice, "If you tell, I will hurt you and your sisters and brother, do you understand?"

Girl, I was shaking in fear after he said it. I could only nod my head in a suggestion of yes. Honestly, after what he'd done to me already, I believed anything at that point. I genuinely was worried about me and my sisters and my little brother. So I kept quiet about that night, and the next day he told us that it was okay to go outside to play.

This was an odd thing to say because Mom told us that it was not safe out there. I looked at my sisters as if "well, maybe it's okay," and I went next-door to see if the kids could come out to play with us too.

They were the same age as we were, so we all stayed in the playground area in the middle where there were only two swings that worked. The playground also had one slide and two seesaws that worked. It felt good to be outside, so we just started playing and laughing.

Then, this teenage boy came and started sliding and playing on the monkey bars. He came over to us, and he asked if we wanted some candy. Now, if you ask young kids if they want candy, do you imagine any child turning down that offer? No, and this boy knew it.

Girl, who would have thought, a stranger would use another kid to lure other younger children away from their home, all so he could do harm and awful things to them. This boy said to us, "If you want candy, then come with me."

Most of the kids said, "Okay," but I asked, "Why do we have to follow you? Don't you have it right now?"

"I did, but I gave away what I had to the other kids, but I only live down the street, so just come with me." He started walking away, and we all looked at each other. We began following him until we noticed he began to walk too far away from our house. After about a block, we all stopped walking behind him and asked, "Where do you live?"

"We are almost there." He continued to walk, and at that moment, the other kids turn around to go back to our house. I said to them, "Hey, I thought you guys wanted some candy? He said that he wasn't that far, so come on guys, it's going to be okay; once we get it, we can go."

While they kept walking back to our house, one of the next-door kids stood there watching me as I continued walking with this boy into his apartment. After about five or ten minutes, the teenage boy ran out of the apartment that he took me to.

The neighbor kid who watched me go in behind him ran back to my house; at the same time, my sister and the other kids began telling our parents, "This older boy was taking us to his apartment to give us candy, but we turned around to come back, but Connie kept walking with him to his apartment."

Then my mom said, "Why were you guys outside in the first place? And why did this boy offer you guys candy and then told you to follow him to his apartment?"

My sister said, "He asked us if we wanted some candy, and we said yes. Then he said we have to follow him to his house, and that's when we all followed him. But we didn't want to follow him anymore, but Connie said she was going to go and get the candy for us, but she never came out, Mommy."

Mom called out for Fat, and he came from the back of the house, asking, "What is going on?"

Mom said, "The kids said that this older boy took Connie to his apartment to supposedly get some candy for the kids, but the kids decided to come back to tell someone about this boy. My daughter is still with him. Please explain to me what the hell were you thinking, Fat, sending them outside unsupervised when I told you how dangerous this neighborhood is."

Fat said to my sister and the other kids, "Can you remember where he took you guys?"

"Yes. He took us down there," and they all begin pointing toward the teenage boy's house.

My stepdad said to them, "Let's go, and Ruby, just stay here until we get back. I promise I'll bring her home, and I'm not coming back here without her, okay?"

They all took the elevator down to the main floor, and Fat told the kids to get into his car so they could show Fat which way to go. As my stepdad drove up to the teenage boy's place, the one kid who stood there watching said, "That's where he took her, right there."

As my stepdad started to get out of the car, he told them, "Do not unlock these doors until I get back, okay?" They agreed.

He walked up to the door and knocked, but when no one answered, he kicked the door down. When he went inside, this old man stood at the end of the hallway by a bedroom and as he sees my stepdad. Then Fat noticed that I was laying on top of the kitchen table, tied to it.

My stepdad ran back to where this old white man was and started beating him, yelling, "What the hell are you doing with my daughter? When I'm finished with you, I promise you will never kidnap another child, you sick old bastard. Tell me what you were planning on doing with her, you sick fuck. Tell me."

The old white man had given me some Kool-Aid to drink, and it made me very drowsy. All I could hear was this man saying, "Please don't kill me."

After my stepdad finished beating the hell out of this white man, he took the rope off me, grabbed me, and then we went to the car and headed back to our house.

When we got back, Mom asked, "What happened? Oh my God, I'm so happy that you found my daughter." At that moment, she started crying, saying, "Fat, why did you send them outside in the first place when you know how dangerous it is living here in Chicago, especially when they are not being looked after while they are outside. Were you trying to see if something would happen to my children? Well, now you know, and if something had happened to her, my parents would not let me live it down. What you did was crazy, Fat! Did you call the police when you got to the apartment so that they can arrest this man, at least?"

My stepdad said, "No, I just beat the hell out of him, and then I grab my stepdaughter and left." And while the two of them talked about what happened, Girl, my heart was still beating very fast.

After we got home, I knew for the first time that dangerous people were out there. Yet, I know for a fact that we are not alone in this world because a higher power must have been watching over me that day. Within minutes this crazy white man would have killed me, and I wouldn't be here to share my story. I believe that was the first-time danger stared me in the face as a child.

After about a week, my stepdad took us back outside so that we could show him what this boy looks like. When we saw him, we pointed and shouted to our stepdad, "That's him!"

Our stepdad grabbed this boy up by his jacket and told him, "If you ever lure any more children away from their house for a stranger again, it will be the last time you will ever do it. If not, you will be the next one to come up missing."

Girl, when I heard my stepdad say that to this boy, I believed what he was saying because I saw evil in his eye as he held this boy in the air. When he put the boy down, he ran away fast without looking back and with good reason. At that moment, I believed I was introduced to Satan, that day who lived in our home as my stepdad.

3: LEAVING CHICAGO

Shortly after that, my mom moved away from that neighborhood and into the Cabrini-Green housing project in Chicago. Trust me when I say it wasn't any better living there. I thought to myself, "Could my nightmare get any worse?" Moving into the project offered a whole new set of nightmares for a young child at the age of six.

On our first day of school, which was not extremely far from our house, a block at the most, my older sister and I were chased home by some bad kids who seemed to be angry at us because we looked better than them. Later that day, I heard my stepdad talking to our mom about the gang members that lived in the projects. Believe me, after I heard him say that it made me even more afraid to go to school the next day.

So the next morning, when Mom came in to get us up for school, I played like I was too sick to go, and she asked me, "Baby, why is you pretending to be sick?"

I said, "Because yesterday after those bad kids chased us all the way home, they told us that they are going to beat us tomorrow when we go back to school. And they told us that we were too Miss Goody-Two-Shoes and that we don't belong there at their school. One of them grabbed me by my hair and pulled it really hard, and she tore my shirt."

"Honey, they are just miserable children who are probably not getting enough attention at home from their parents. They are just looking to take it out on good sweet kids like you and your sister. You guys are the newbies on the block, which is why they are picking on you two. You're just the new kids in the neighborhood, is all."

Girl, I'm not sure if this was supposed to make me feel better about going to school that morning or not, but it didn't. My sister and I were still too afraid to go to school, so my mom ended up taking us to school and talking to the principal about the children chasing us home the previous day. The principal told my mom that he would talk with their parents. It must have worked because after school that day, we didn't have to run home.

That weekend my crazy stepdad waited for nightfall before he went out and attacked one of the gang members in that area. And of course, this only made the gang angrier; at the same time, I believed my stepdad was trying to show them that he was not afraid to stand up against bullies.

I overheard my stepdad and his brother talking in the living room about it, the leader of the gang was trying to recruit my stepdad's brother to join the gang, which is why my stepdad decided to go after one of their gang members.

All this did was light the fuel on an already bad situation, and these gang members found out Fat attacked one of their guys. On Monday, one of the gang member's younger relatives picked on us that day after school. And Girl, this went on for a while, us running home from school.

One day my mom's younger brother Jeff who was in his twenties at the time and didn't take mess from anybody, came to stay with us.

On the day he arrived, the older gang member saw my uncle Jeff while he was walking us to school. And, as we were coming home from school, one of those bad kids went to tell his brother that we had our uncle walking with us. That evening when my uncle was taking the trash out, one of the gang members got off the elevator.

After my uncle placed the trash bag into the bin, the gang member said to him, "I heard that you are new in our area, which means you either have to join us or leave the area, which is it going to be?"

My uncle said, "I want to be doing neither of them, and if you think for one second that you can intimidate me and my family well, I got news for you I'm here to stay and to protect my family."

As my uncle stared into this gang member's eyes with the look of fierce power, the gang member just shook his head as if to say "okay," and he then pushed the elevator button to go down. As the elevator doors opened, the gang member got on and locked eyes with my uncle as the door closed.

Girl, that evening around four-o'clock, that gang member from earlier came to our door with three more gang members. They knocked so hard on the door my uncle Jeff said to us, "I want you kids to go in your bedrooms and don't come out until I come and tell you to, okay?"

We went back to our rooms and closed the doors like he told us. My uncle got two of mom's big cooking pots, put water in them and added some grits. When the gang member continued to bang on the door, Uncle Jeff said to them, "If you don't get away from my house, you will regret it."

After about twenty-five minutes, the next thing I heard was my uncle saying to the main guy, "I dare you to step over my door line if you think you are bad enough."

Sure enough, when that guy started to step over the line into our house, my uncle hauled off and hit him as hard as he could. As he fell backward onto the ground, my uncle dared the other gang member to come in. And, Girl, all I can say is thank the Lord this was before gangs began carrying firearms.

After about a second, the other gang members thought my uncle was tougher than they were. As two of them saw the main gang member lying there on the ground, they must have started thinking if they try to attack my uncle, he'd probably knock them to the ground too. My uncle then said, "If you don't leave right now, it will get worse, so I suggest you get the hell out of here now. If I hear that you or any of your gang members hurt my family again, it will be the last time."

Girl, these guys just left after that. Oh my God, it was so cool that my uncle stood up against them for us. Even though my uncle told us to stay in our room, I snuck out to see what was going on. I couldn't believe what I just witnessed with those guys! I was in shock after watching my uncle knock their leader on his butt. He showed them that he was not afraid of them.

After they left, my uncle closed the door. As he did, I ran back to the bedroom so he wouldn't know I watched. Minutes later, he came back to our bedroom and told us to come out. I said, "Uncle, I saw you knock that guy out, and he hit the ground."

We all came into the living room and saw some blood on the ground in front of the door. I also noticed that my uncle didn't use the two big pots filled with hot water and grits. My uncle called our grandparents and told them what he had just done to protect us, and of course, my grandparents said, "What? I want you to tell Ruby that you are bringing our grandchildren back to Carbondale to stay with us until she gets herself together. That place is not a safe place to raise kids. When she comes home, tell her to call me right away. Do you hear me, Jeff?"

My uncle said, "Yes, Mom. I heard you; I'll tell her as soon as she gets home, and I'm sure that she's not going to be happy about your decision, Mom, but I'll give her your message."

When my uncle ended the call with our grandma, I had such a big smile on my face because it was the best news I had heard in a long time, especially after experiencing the violence and abuse with my stepdad.

I truly felt God was watching over me because, for a while, I was starting to think that God didn't care, but now things were looking up. As a child, when you begin to see more evil than good, it causes you to wonder if this is what God planned for your life. I believe it was God who sent my uncle Jeff to Chicago to keep us safe from evil because he showed up at the right time to protect us from those gang bangers.

This is what I want to share with you, Girl. God teaches us in his Bible against evildoers, according to the Book of Psalm 144:1: "Of David Blessed be the Lord, my rock who trains my hands for war and my fingers for battle." We have to stand up for our family; otherwise, the people who are filled with evil will continue thinking that they can do harm and get away with it.

I'm not saying that we should carry guns. That's not what I'm saying at all. What I am saying is with God on our side, we will always have his powerful Archangel watching over us. God's word in the Book of Isaiah 41:10 says to us, "Fear not, for I am with you; be not dismayed, for I am your God; I will strengthen you, I will help you, I will uphold you with my righteous right hand."

I knew that God loved me. So when my mom came home that evening, my uncle Jeff told her what happened several hours before, about fighting off the leader of the gangbangers. After he finished explaining to her what happened, he said to Mom, "Look, big sis, I spoke with Mom and Dad right after it happened. And, well, Sis, they wasn't too happy that the kids are living in fear here in Chicago. Mom told me to tell you that she wants me to bring the kids to stay with them until you get things together in your life. Also, Sis, after what I experienced today, I too agree with Mom and Dad. It's not safe for the kids to live here in Chicago anymore. Now, if I hadn't shown up here when I did, who knows what may have happened to these kids. Would you have continued to allow your kids to run home from school every day until one of those bad kids hurt Connie or Cookie?"

Mom said, "Well, I will admit that Chicago is not a place for them, but Mom and Dad told me never to come to them for any help, which is why I stay with Fat because he's helping me keep a roof over our head. I know that he has some emotional and anger issues that he has with his family, but he does love me and cares about the kids, Jeff."

Girl, see, here's where I thought my mom was delusional. Our stepdad did not love or care for us, which is why it took me so long to forgive my mother. However, I do believe my mom had convinced herself that my stepdad was a good man. Maybe it's because he was helping her by providing for her and her children, but what I can't figure out is how she concluded that he loved her kids. I'm still scratching my head on this one.

And Girl, right here is where I want to share that we, as women, don't have to feel desperate to the point that our children's lives are in jeopardy of hidden sexual predators. Trust me, hundreds of them are out there who have not been charged with a sexual crime.

Right after Mom finished making excuses for my stepdad, my uncle said to her, "Well, Mom and Dad have clearly changed their minds now, so why not give them this opportunity to help you with the kids? I'll take them back with me this weekend; they already said that they would wire me enough money for all of the kids."

Mom answered, "Okay, that's fine, but let them know that as soon as I get myself together, and decide if I'm going to stay with Fat, I'll be back home to find a place for all of us. I'm sure Fat won't like it, but at this point, this gives him a chance to get some help with his issues."

Girl, after she told my uncle yes, we left that weekend. I was in a state of shock when she agreed, and at the same time, filled with joy. So, our uncle Jeff drove us to his house, and Mom made sure our school records were transferred to Carbondale so that we could start school after arriving there.

Girl, it was the best day of my life when we left Chicago. I was especially grateful that we were not living with our stepdad anymore. It was such a relief to know that he couldn't hurt us again. Living with him was like living with Satan, and the thing is, my mom thought he was a good man to her and her kids. Little did she know that he took out his anger on us kids all the time.

4: THE 911 CALL

Once we settled in Carbondale and a couple of years go by, my mom finally found her way to Carbondale. She left Fat, and once she settled herself in Carbondale, she found a night job and got her own place.

My grandparents helped her until she was able to do it herself because they loved their older daughter and wanted to be a part of their grandkids' lives. The house she rented was not too far from our elementary school, which was nice for us. We could walk home from school with friends without being chased by violent kids like in Chicago. Everything was going well.

Six months went by after Mom moved to be near us, and low and behold, our evil stepdad found out where we lived. I couldn't believe it. One afternoon when we got home from school, I heard a knock on the door. Mom went to the door, and when she opened it, I thought to myself, "Oh, know it's my stepdad. How did he find out where we live? I heard she had been communicating with him without telling her parents or us since she's been here."

Girl, I was about eight-years-old now, and here comes evil walking back into our lives again. After seeing the look of fear in Mom's eyes, and her facial expression, I whispered the words, "Oh, God, help us."

I believed she was just as surprised as we all were to see him at our doorstep, and at the same time, I couldn't tell if she was acting excited to see him because she was afraid of him or if she was happy to see him.

I'm sure she felt terrified that he was there, and of course, after dinner that night, I heard him yelling at her, "Why did you lie to me, Ruby? You told me that you were coming here to pick up the kids and return to Chicago, so when I didn't hear from you after six months, I had to find out from one of your girlfriends that you were staying here in Carbondale, that you had found a job and gotten your own place. Now I'm telling you right now, woman, that you are going to pack these kids up and head back to Chicago with me."

Mom said to him, "Fat, you know that I can't just pack up and take my children out of school, not without my parents noticing it and not to mention they know that we are not together anymore. How would it look if I go and take the kids out of school and especially when the school administrator will contact my parents first? I'm sorry that I lied to you, but let's face it, Fat, you were too abusive to my kids, and they are afraid of you because of it. I don't think it's a great idea for us to be together anymore, Fat. I won't force my kids to love you or not be afraid of you, which means that this idea of me and the kids coming back to live with you again in Chicago is not realistic."

"No, I know you can't make the kids love me or want to come back with us, but what I do expect from you is for you to be a mother and take charge of your children because you are their mother, and you should be in control of them, not your parents, Ruby."

"Fat, that's how you were brought up, but that's not how my parents raised me. They gave us a choice, and I'm not going to force my kids to go back to Chicago if they don't want to, and I'm not going against my parents."

My stepdad continues, "It's time for you to stand up to them and tell them that you love me and that I'm good for you and those kids."

Girl, all I was thinking was, "God, please give my mom the strength to stand up to my stepdad, and don't let her take us back to that hell-hole place."

Then I heard my mom say, "Fat; look, this isn't as easy as you think it is just to take them out of school and pick up and go back to Chicago. Especially when my parents paid for everything here, which means I can't leave right now."

I was so happy to hear that she was standing up for herself to my stepdad!

She continued, "I need more time, Fat, because my parents helped me get a job here, and I need to stay here to show them that I am responsible enough as an adult. My parents are right about one thing, my children did not ask to be here in this world, and I'm not going to leave them on my parents. I'm not going to take my kids back to Chicago. Not after what my parents have done. And, the kids really like it here. These kids, for the first time, have made friends, and they're so happy being here close to their grandparents. Right now, I have to get ready for work, and in a few minutes, Jenna is coming over to watch the kids for me. I don't think it's a good idea for you to stay here while I'm at work. When I get home tonight, I'll call you. Maybe you should get a hotel room while you are here, Fat."

"So now you don't trust me with the kids?"

"Fat, being that you just appeared out of nowhere, I don't think it's a good idea for you to watch them tonight is all I'm saying."

He tried to sweet-talk Mom into giving him another chance. Mom had a trusting heart and believed in giving people another chance to prove her wrong. She fell for his sweet-talk and said, "Fat, I'll give you a chance to prove me wrong and let you stay tonight only, but you will need to get yourself a hotel room if you are planning on being here longer then this weekend. So, I'll call Jenna and tell her not to come over tonight."

After my mom left for work, my stepdad was in the kitchen fixing dessert for us to eat. Afterward, he asked us if we wanted to play a game called hide-and-go-seek. He said to me, "Rabbit, you and the girls go and hide, and your little brother will come and find you guys, okay?"

I was still so afraid of him that I said, "Okay." All of a sudden, that fear I had back in Chicago came rushing back to me. I had this feeling in the pit of my stomach that something bad was going to happen, especially since we are alone with him again.

Girl, when I got outside, I went over to my older sister Cookie. I said to her, "I don't feel good about this game, and I don't trust him with our little brother. Should I go back in there?"

Cookie said, "What if he gets mad and starts beating us for coming back into the house when he told us to go outside?" We were too young to stand up to him. I was eight, and Cookie was nine, and not to mention that we both were scared.

At that moment, I walked past the back door of the house and saw my stepdad giving my little brother something to drink. Afterward, he blindfolded my little brother, turned him around three times, and pointed him toward the back door to find us. I started calling my little brother in a low voice, "Ricky, follow my voice come over to me. I'm over here, listen to me, okay?"

When he came over to me, I smelled rubbing alcohol on his breath, and I knew something was wrong with him. Oh my God, Girl, at that very second, I said a prayer to God, "Please help my little brother and us right now, Heavenly Father, keep us from my evil stepdad. Amen." Shortly after my prayer, God moved on my heart. My intuition was clear, and I knew what I should do.

I went over to my older sister Cookie, and I said to her, "Something is wrong with Ricky; I believe Fat made him drink some rubbing alcohol because I can smell it on his breath. One of us needs to go over to our neighbor's house and ask her to call grandpa. I think you should do it! That way, I can stay here and watch our little brother."

My sister asked, "No, why can't you do it?"

Now my older sister never was a brave kind of person when it came to standing up for herself, so I said to her, "Fine, I'll go, but you need to keep playing as if we are still hiding until I get back with help."

Girl, I knew if my stepdad caught me over to our neighbor's house, he would beat me to death, but for some reason, I felt the strength of God come over me. I began walking next door to Mrs. Smith's house. I knocked on the door, and she answered, "Who is it?"

"My name is Connie, and something is wrong with my little brother. Can you call my granddaddy?"

"Oh, Honey, come in. Are you Ruby's daughter?"

"Yes, ma'am. Can you call my grandpa because my little brother drank something bad?"

"Let me look up their phone number in the white pages, or do you know it?"

"Yes, ma'am, I do because my grandparents made us memorize it in case of emergency."

"Let me dial it for you, Sweetie, and I'll hand it to you after they pick up. Where is your mommy?"

I said, "She's at work, and my stepdad is watching us. He gave my little brother something to drink, and I believe it was rubbing alcohol."

"Oh, my God! Then you are not going back over there until I get your grandparents on the phone." After the call connected, she began talking to my grandparents. I heard her tell them that I was at her house and that I'd told her something was wrong with my little brother, and I believed her stepdad gave him something bad to drink.

She then gave me the phone, and I said, "Hi Granddaddy. Mom is at work, and Fat is at our house. He gave Ricky some rubbing alcohol to drink."

Right away, my grandpa said, "I'll be right there, Sweetie, so give the phone back to Mrs. Smith, okay?"

And the next thing I knew, I heard Mrs. Smith say to my grandpa, "I'll call 911 over to your daughter Ruby's house right away."

When emergency help showed up at our house, I saw my grandpa pull up right beside the ambulance. Girl, my grandpa was so mad at my mom for letting my stepdad back into her life again.

Of course, as soon as my stepdad heard the ambulance pull up, he looked out the window. Then he saw the police behind the ambulance. When the paramedics went up to our house to knock on the door, Fat ran out the back door.

My sister Cookie answered the door, and right away, the paramedics saw my little brother laying on the couch, and they began looking into his eyes. They told my grandpa if they didn't get there when they did, it could have led to his death because drinking rubbing alcohol has bad effects on the nervous system.

Girl, after my grandpa heard that, he got even angrier at my mom, and he said to us, "I'm taking you guys with me over to my house for now." I was so glad to hear grandpa say that!

Then I said, "Grandpa, I heard Fat telling Mom that he wanted her to stand up to her parents and to demand that she take us back to Chicago with him."

My granddad replied, "Oh, he did? Well, he has another thing coming if he thinks that he is taking you guys back to Chicago with him, and if Ruby thinks that I'm going to allow her to take you guys back there, we'll make sure that she will never get her hands on you guys again."

Now, while we were at our grandparent's house, my little brother was lying in the hospital. When my mom finally got home from work, she walked up to the house, and of course, my stepdad opened the door.

Girl, his ass had circled back around to the house, after running away from the ambulance and police. When my mother went into the house, Fat says to her, "Your dad was here, and he took the kids with him back to their house, I suppose."

"Why was he here, Fat?" She asked. "What did you do now, and please do not lie to me because I'm sure my parents will tell me."

Fat was an evil man because he tried to convince my mom that my little brother must have drunk the rubbing alcohol, thinking it was water. Now, why would a little child take some rubbing alcohol and drink it voluntarily? I don't think so. I knew if my mom fell for this, then she is weak in my eyes.

Fat told her, "It must have been one of your kids who went over to the neighbor's house to call the ambulance. When they got here, I looked out the window, and that's when I saw the police as well as your dad, and I ran out the back door."

Confused, Mom asked, "Fat, why would they need to go over to the neighbor's house? Again, I ask you, what did you do to cause them to go to the neighbor's house?"

He replied, "I let the kids go outside to play a game of hide-and-go-seek, and like I said, Ricky must have drunk some rubbing alcohol by mistake, thinking that it was water. You know how kids can be, especially when they are young, and you know that I wouldn't hurt your kids."

Mom said, "Of course I know how kids can mistake something for being water, but the thing is, my father will not believe that is what happened."

Girl, you see, right there is where my mom should have told my stepdad, "Fat, for one thing, my child wouldn't drink rubbing alcohol, and for another, they can smell the difference from water or rubbing alcohol no matter how young they are because I use it on them when they get a cut or a scratch." But she didn't say that.

This world is filled with so much evil, and people who aren't close to God or even make him a part of their lives are open for Satan to possess their soul. According to God, as found in the Book of 1 Thessalonians 5:22 ESV: "Abstain from every form of evil."

Even though my mom was trying to be strong, her flesh was weak. My stepdad had control over her, I believe, because of her weakness for him, all because she thought that she couldn't take care of herself.

Girl, what I am saying here is, be strong and have confidence in yourself. Love comes from within you, and love will find you according to God's word when he says in the Book of Matthew 26: 41 ESV: "Watch and pray that you may not enter into temptation. The Spirit indeed is willing, but the flesh is weak."

That weekend my stepdad tells mom that she needs to go over to her parents' house and bring her kids home. The last time my mom had spoken to her parents was after that horrible event that happened, and she knew where she stood with her parents far as that went.

I couldn't believe Fat told her to go over there and demand them to turn us over to her. It wasn't enough that he tried to kill my little brother; this crazy man was serious when he told mom to get us, so the two of them could take off for Chicago.

Of course, mom calls her parents to explain that ridiculous story Fat told her, and once my grandparents heard it, they said, "Ruby, what has gotten over you? Do you really believe this story that he has told you? Why I cannot believe that you can't see how seriously crazy this man is. If you do not divorce this man, I'm afraid he will end up killing one of your children or you for that matter."

My grandma continued, "How did he know where you live? And, more importantly, why have you let this man back into your life after what he's done to these kids? I really believe you have lost your mind, Ruby."

Mom still tried to sell the story to her parents even after they told her that they didn't believe it. After mom hung up the phone with her parents, Fat told her that after dark, they'd go over to her parents and load us kids in the car, and the two of them would head to Chicago. Mom actually went into her parent's house, walked into the bedroom where we were, and she began telling us to get up and get dressed.

Right away, I said, "Mom, why? Grandpa said we're not going anywhere with you or Fat."

Meanwhile, Grandpa and Grandma came out of their bedroom. Mom stood there; I was lying in bed, and Mom saw her parents open the bedroom door. At this point, Grandpa is furious with my mom. I can hear it in his tone.

He said, "Ruby, these kids have no reason to just make up a story like that. Why would they? They are terrified of the man, so you tell me why they would create something as serious as this. Do you even know the whole story of what really happened? Or are you just going to rely on what Fat told you? Before your son came out of the house, your daughter Connie saw Fat hand him a cup, which was the rubbing alcohol, and then he blindfolded Ricky. After turning him a few times, he sent him outside to find the other kids. Fat thought it was funny to see that child stumbling around looking for his sisters. Now, how sick is that, Ruby? And this is the man who told you that he loves your kids."

Then Grandma said, "If it wasn't for our brave granddaughter going over to the neighbor's house to ask her to call us grandparents, no telling if your son would be alive. That's when Mrs. Smith told your dad that something is wrong with our grandson. After hearing that, your dad went over to your house right away. At the same time, Mrs. Smith called 911. The first responders got there in time to save your son's life; otherwise, he would have died. Now I don't know what this crazy man has over you, but you are not getting your hands on these kids anymore, Ruby."

Right then, Grandpa cut in and said, "Ruby, are you using drugs? Because for the life of me, I can't figure why you would let this man back into your life after what your brother Jeff and your sister Genola have told us about this man. Genola told us how Fat threw her down a flight of stairs when she stayed with you there in Chicago. And how he's been beating on the kids whenever you aren't there, and I'm almost sure he's done other things to them as well. Otherwise, why would these kids be so afraid of him? Right now, Ruby, I'm so ashamed to call you my daughter."

Girl, mom was speechless after hearing what her parents said about her husband. Grandpa continued, "If you want to follow this man to hell, then you go right ahead, but I will not allow you to take my grandkids there with you; they will be staying here with me and your mother, and we will manage with these kids. And I'm sure with the help of your siblings, the kids will be better off with us. They will have a good life growing up here with us. Next time, if you come back, you better be done with Fat. Otherwise, you will never get these kids back, Ruby."

Girl, I have never heard my grandpa say a curse word before until that night. Mom didn't know what to say after both her parents told her that she wasn't going to take us with her.

Eventually, she said, "Okay, I know you both think the worst of me right now, but Fat is going through a rough time in his life right now with his own mother and dad. I know that you guys don't believe me, but he just recently found out who his real dad is, and therefore he is hurting mentally. Plus, his dad enlisted in the army, and while he was there, he got a few pieces of bullet fragments in the back of his head. Fat's had too many people walk out of his life. I know you and mom think that I'm crazy for wanting to be with him, but I'm not. It's because you raised me to love my husband, as the Bible says in the Book of Ephesians 5:22 ESV: 'Wives, submit to your own husband, as to the Lord.'" Mom continued, "Isn't that what you taught us, Mom?"

Then my grandma said, "Yes, but we also taught you not to be a complete fool, Ruby. And you also missed the part when it states in the Book of Colossians 3:18-19 ESV: 'Wives, submit to your husbands, as is fitting in the Lord. Husbands, love your wives, and do not be harsh with them.'"

Now Girl, if mom were trying to get into a Bible war with her mother, then I'm afraid she would lose that one; because Grandma carried her Bible morning, noon and night. Mom continued, "He's not as bad of a man as it seems, and I do love him. I will stand by him because he needs me. Which is why I want to move back to Chicago so I can help him get through his emotional issues."

Grandma replied, "Ruby, what kind of emotional issues is he dealing with? All that I can see is he has some mental problems, and you can't help anyone like that. He needs to be admitted into a mental hospital so that he can get the real help that he needs."

In Fat's defense, Mom said, "He's been trying to work through it. I'm sorry that I've allowed him to take it out on my kids, but he's not a bad person. Now, what if you found out that your parents had kept horrible secrets from you? Wouldn't you want dad to be there for you?"

Grandpa countered, "Ruby, this still doesn't give him the right to beat you or your kids or anyone else for that matter. I'm not buying this bullshit; I'm still not allowing you to take my grandkids through this anymore."

Grandma chimed in, "Ruby, I'm sorry that happened to him, but I wouldn't let my children go through what this man has put them through. Not even if I loved him, therefore, I agree with your father on this one."

Grandpa followed with, "Your mom and I both believe that you can do whatever you want with this man, but you will leave the kids with us until you come to your senses." Right after my grandparents walked Mom to the front door, they went back to bed.

After about twenty minutes went by, I heard someone come into the house. At first, I thought it was Uncle Jeff, but of course, I heard my stepdad's voice talking to Mom.

"Get the kids up so we can get on the road toward Chicago. These are your kids, not your parents' kids. This means you are a grown-ass woman, and we are taking them with us tonight, Ruby."

Mom pleaded, "I don't think we should, Fat. I think we should leave the kids here now, and we can go back to Chicago. We can start finding you a counselor because that's the only way I can get the kids back from my parents. Fat, they are not going to give me the kids as long as you have anger issues, can't you see that? Let's leave right now before my parents hear us."

THE 911 CALL

At that moment, Girl, I heard my granddad's voice and the sound of his shotgun. He yelled, "Over my dead body will I let you walk out of here with my grandkids."

I saw my uncle Johnny coming down the stairs. I thought he'd gone to his Girlfriend's house, but I guess not because he grabbed Fat and started beating him. Then Uncle Johnny told him, "If you ever put your hands on any one of these children again, I will kill you."

Next, my grandpa said to Fat, "I'm giving you five seconds to get the hell out of my house, or I'll blow your head clean off. Leave right now."

Girl, my mom was standing over us, saying to my stepdad, "Let's go now, Fat before my father shoots you," and then the two of them left.

Right after they left, my granddad called the police to report the issue. When the police arrived at their house, Grandma opened the door, and the officer asked, "What seems to be the problem here, Ma'am?"

My granddad came to the door to explain the incident to the officer. He said, "My older daughter is Ruby, and her husband tried to poison our grandson the other night. Tonight he came into my home trying to take the kids. I believe he's driving to Chicago tonight. When I told him to leave my house and he would not, I pulled my shotgun on him. That's the moment my daughter told him that they should leave, and that's when we call 911."

The officer asked, "Do you have the ambulance and hospital paperwork to back up what you are stating?"

Grandma went into the dining room, opened the china cabinet drawer, and got the hospital and the ambulance paperwork to give to the officer.

Meanwhile, the officer asked, "Where is he now; do you know?"

"He's at my daughter Ruby's house probably," Grandpa said. "I overheard her say they are going back to Chicago tonight, and I'm not sure if they left yet, but I'll write down her address."

"Sure, that would be great," said the officer, "I'll go by there and speak with him. What is his full name? Do you know it?"

Grandma volunteered, "His full name is Erstin McCloud, I believe."

"Would you happen to have his address in Chicago?"

Grandpa answered, "We don't have any address for him, officer. Is there some kind of restraining order that we can get in place to keep him from coming back to our house again?"

The officer said to my grandparents, "You can go down to the court and ask to speak to the judge about getting a restraining order in place against your son-in-law based on the hospital paperwork and the police report number that I'm about to give you now. You just be sure to give them this number and the hospital paperwork, which will show how damaging this man is to your grandchildren. I am sure the judge will grant you a restraining order. After all, you are their grandparents, plus you have a good standing here in Carbondale since you've lived here for quite a while and own your property."

Girl, on Monday morning, Grandma and Grandpa went to the county courthouse to file a restraining order against my stepdad, and the judge gave my grandparent's the protection order as well as the restraining order. This meant my stepdad could not come within seven feet of my grandparent's property or our school, and if he violated it, the order states he would be arrested on the scene. I was so happy after my grandparents got that restraining order!

My grandparents were getting older, and yet they still took us into their house. I knew it was going to be a challenge for them, but their other children called to offer help, and they were relieved. My mom's sister and brother were not too surprised when she chose to run off with Fat instead of staying and raising her children.

We all had to be split up to make it easy on Grandma and Grandpa. My sister Edwina and I stayed with our grandparents, and my older sister and younger sister went with Mom's older brother Buddy. Ricky, my little brother, stayed with Mom's middle brother Johnny after he got out of the hospital.

Girl, I do believe that as a young child, God was trying to get my attention. Because of what I'd gone through, God knew anger was taking shape within my heart. He also saw that forgiveness was going to be a challenge for me. So, as I started attending Sunday school and learning about forgiveness, I didn't completely understand the whole meaning behind forgiveness because I was too young still. Why would a child understand or know what it means to forgive?

Right, Girl, wouldn't you agree? Understanding only comes when you get older and begin experiencing things in life. As a child, I didn't know that when we don't forgive those who hurt us, life begins to get tough from the choices we make. It's one of God's way of getting our attention.

Through our challenges and when we are rebellious, my grandma would say to me, "God has his way of allowing us to go through things to lead us where we are supposed to be in our lives. Challenges make us stronger."

Girl, I was still learning and trying to understand what God wants from me and what's my whole purpose for being here on earth, and whenever I went to church with my grandma, I wanted to know everything about the Bible so that I would get the whole meaning of forgiveness.

At the same time, I couldn't understand why my mom would choose to leave her kids for a husband who would abuse her children. For my whole life, I held on to this anger because it didn't make any sense to me as a young child.

5: BROTHER BETRAYAL

After about four years, when I was twelve, Mom did return to Carbondale. I still couldn't forgive her for leaving us. She finally saw that our stepdad wasn't going to change into the person she hoped he'd become. He had too much hate and evil in his heart toward his family.

Of course, she had two boys by him before she left him, and let me tell you, Girl, if my uncle hadn't gone to Chicago and gotten us when he did, I'm not sure what would have happened to all of us. My uncle Jeff saved us from my evil stepdad that year; I truly believed we would have ended up beaten to death.

Even though Mom was back, my grandma continued taking us to church. Over the years of being mistreated by my stepdad and different men that my mom brought around me as a child and as a teenager, the hate and anger began to take shape inside my heart. It was almost like God timed it just right for my grandparents to take us into their lives.

I believe God was preparing me for the road ahead of me. As a young girl, I didn't even know the Book of Matthew had scriptures on forgiveness. These scriptures turned out to be the most challenging for me.

I never knew how God would test me as an adult, and of course, it took me many years to really understand what God meant by his word on forgiveness. According to Matthew 6:14-15: "For if you forgive other people when they sin against you, your heavenly Father will also forgive you. But if you do not forgive others their sins, your Father will not forgive your sins."

Girl, I went through hell and back living with my mom and being the second to the oldest child. And, I know that everyone has a story to tell about their parents and how horrible it must have been growing up in their household at one point or another. Still, at the same time, if you haven't walked in that person's shoes, you can't possibly know what kind of hell they went through until you have shared their pain with them.

My childhood was like living in a nightmare zone, and I couldn't get out of it. I believe God also showed me that although my mom had her faults, she was learning as everyone else does here on this earth. There were rumors before I came into this evil world that my mom was raped by her own uncle on granddad's side of the family.

Even though it took me some time to forgive my mother for how she raised me, God brought me through life challenges so that I could see why it's important to forgive those who hurt me. I must say, from the accumulation of pain I've endured for years that I held inside my heart, this was a hard lesson for me.

Once mom got settled in her own place in Carbondale again, Grandma and Grandpa allowed her to take us back, and after about three years later, she gave birth to my younger brother Jwan. Of course, as a girl of only thirteen, she made me responsible for cleaning and cooking as well as raising my other siblings while she partied with her friends.

I'm not sure if Mom was traumatized from the physical abuse that she endured by my stepdad, that led her to drugs, but she started having fish-fry and cookouts on Friday's. I remember men coming over with a bucket full of fish that she would have us kids clean on the front porch.

That is when I met Clyde for the first time; he would come over for the cookout and play cards at the kitchen table while mom was at the stove cooking catfish in one pan and simmering a pot of spaghetti on the other burner. Friday's were the first time I got a break from cooking each week. These Friday evening cookouts went on for a while, throughout our lives as teenagers, with men coming over every Friday evening with fresh fish for us kids to clean.

During that summer, I started liking this teenage guy named Sam from high school. Girl, for the first time, I was beginning to have fun with my friends. We teenagers would hang out at the park by the high school on the weekends. And of course, Sam was there as well, and we were together.

I was happy because he was my first boyfriend in high school, and he was such a kind and gentle person. Sam played football, and I played soccer; he started inviting me over to his house after practice on the weekends, and on weekdays after practice, the two of us would walk home after school together. I enjoyed spending time with him at his house, and his mom and younger sister were so nice.

One day I went over to see Sam, and his mother, Patricia, asked me, "Sweetie, I know you like my son a lot, but I just want to be sure that you are smart when it comes to having sex; are you on the pill?"

I answered, "No, ma'am, but Sam and I have decided that we wanted to wait until we finish with high school and go to college before having sex."

"Well, that's really great news to hear because there's no hurry to give up your virginity until you are ready."

As Patricia was about to finish our conversation, Sam walked in and said, "Oh, hi, I didn't hear you come in. How long have you been here?"

I said, "Not long, I just got here, and I was just saying hello to your mom."

His mother says to him, "Okay, dear, I'm on my way out for a while, but I'll be back in a little bit. I love you." As she kissed him on his cheek, she says, "Sam I believe she is a keeper. I like her."

Sam answered, "Okay, Mom," then he asked me, "Do you want to go up to my room?"

I agreed, and as we began walking upstairs, I said, "Hey, your mom ask if I was on the pill, and I told her that I am not because you and I decided not to have sex until we both finish high school and go off to college."

He replied, "Oh, did she? She's just making sure that we are being safe because she wants me to play pro-football after college. She means well, and I'm glad you feel the same way as I do about education, and that's why I like you a lot and now so do my mom."

Once we got to his room, I asked, "So what do you want to do?"

"I like to play my football game, but I also have hangman. Do you want to play that instead?"

I said, "Of course I do!"

The game hangman was really popular back then in the seventies. Sam was good at playing it, and I sucked at it because I didn't play as much as he did. While we were playing the game, I saw him glare at me while I focused on beating his ass. So I asked him, "Sam, would you like to kiss me?"

He said, "Yes, if you don't mind."

Sam wasn't the aggressive type of guy, and I liked that about him. As we began to kiss, he started touching my breast, but Sam was also shy, and he stopped to ask, "Is this okay?"

"Yes, it's okay, Sam." As he started caressing my breasts, we paused and agreed that maybe this wasn't a good idea since I wasn't on the pill.

That's when I said to him, "I tell you what, on Monday I'll go after school to the clinic and talk to them about getting some in case. I know that we want to wait, but at the same time, we might want to try it with one another before we go to college. I want to make sure that I can't get pregnant when we do."

Then his brother Sean walked into the room and caught us kissing, and he asked, "What are you two doing in here?"

We both said at the same time, "Nothing." Then we looked at each other, and we went downstairs before his mother came back. As we sat on the couch in the living room, it was beginning to get dark out; so I said to Sam, "Well, I'm going to go now before my mom starts wondering where I am, and I can see it's getting dark out."

His mother just walked in the front door as I was leaving; she asked, "Are you leaving, my dear? I was going to ask if you wanted to stay for dinner."

"Yes, ma'am, I need to get home to help with dinner. But I appreciate you asking me. Thank you."

Sam asked, "Would you like me to walk with you to your house?"

"Sure, I would like that."

As we walked, Sam asked, "I was wondering if you want to be my girlfriend?"

Right after he asked, I tried to be funny by saying, "Well, I kind of thought I was already your girlfriend since we've been hanging out a lot lately. Especially after we started making out in your bedroom a few times."

Sam was one of the most handsome guys in the whole school, plus he played football, which I admired. He smiled and said, "Oh, I see you have a sense of humor. I'm guessing that's a yes? Well, in a sense, I was thinking we were, but I just wanted to make sure."

"Of course, that's a yes! I would love to be your girlfriend. So does this mean that we are officially a couple now?"

Sam answered, "Of course it does; you are now my girl, and you belong to me." I was so happy that he asked me that evening.

After I got home, the drama began. Mom, of course, yelled at me from upstairs, "Where the hell have you been? You were supposed to be home about an hour ago! Get your ass in there and start dinner because I'm about to head out, and I wanted to make sure you got your butt home before I left."

"Remind me, why is this my responsibility again? When you also have an older daughter named Cookie? I am sick of being the only one who is doing anything around here; I have homework to do, Mom. Whether you care or not, I feel more like your servant then your child."

She shouted, "You watch your mouth; you are the only one that I can count on to do a good job around here. I told Cookie to clean the kitchen after you finish cooking; that way, you can get your homework done before you go to bed."

Right before going to bed, I said a prayer, "Heavenly Father, why did you choose my mother and father to be my parents? Please help me understand the reasoning behind it, and most importantly, what is the lesson here?"

Girl, the next morning, as the sun rose, the Holy Spirit spoke and moved on my heart the book of Proverbs 22:6 ESV: "Train up a child in the way he should go, even when he is old, he will not depart from it."

I resented my mother for forcing me to grow up too fast, to do her job instead of allowing me to be a teenager. I knew God had a purpose for why I had to endure all of this even though I didn't like it. On the inside, I felt a strong love from God that gave me the strength to be obedient to my mom.

I woke early the next day to read a few verses from the Bible, and then I roused my siblings and got them dressed in time to catch the bus for school. I actually made it on time myself before the first bell rang for class. As I moved down the hall, I saw Sam going into his classroom. He walked over, kissed me, and asked me, "Do you want to have lunch together today?"

"Yes, I would love that."

During lunch, Sam asked if I wanted to come over again. So, that weekend, on Saturday afternoon, I went to Sam's house. His mom Patricia answered the door, said Sam was not there, but I was welcome to come in and wait for him. She continued to say he was at football practice and usually came straight home after he was done, which meant he should be home in about thirty minutes. As she walked out the door, she told me she'd see me later.

Girl, for some reason, I decided to go up to Sam's room to wait for him. When I got there, I turned on his game box and started playing hangman. Just then, his older brother Sean came into the room. He said, "You do know that Sam is at practice, right?"

I replied, "Yeah, I know because your mom just told me. I knew that; I just forgot, and when your mother answered the door, she told me that it was okay to wait for Sam."

"What game are you playing?" I told him it was hangman. Then Sean came over and sat beside me. Sean was nowhere nearly as polite as his younger brother; he was far more aggressive. He began getting physical with me, and before I knew it, he was on top of me and started kissing me.

I asked Sean to stop and tried to say, "Sean, what are you doing? Please don't do this. I'm with Sam, so please stop." I began crying as I continued pleading with Sean to stop, but he just pulled my panties down and began forcing himself on me.

Sean growled, "Sam is still a boy, and he has no idea how to handle a woman like you. Let's face it; you need a man to show you what you need as a woman. Which is love, and you know this is what you want, isn't it?"

I yelled, "Sean, no, I don't want this! I am with Sam. He's your brother. Don't you care for him enough to not do this to him?" As I lay there, I hoped that some part of him did care enough to know that raping me was wrong. I continued, "Sean, this isn't what you call love; this is called rape. You need to get off of me now!"

After he finished, he said, "No, it isn't rape when you believe in your heart that a person belongs with you, but she just doesn't realize it yet. From the moment I set eyes on you, I felt our souls belonged together, and deep down inside, you felt it too. So you can call this rape all you want, but I know you enjoyed it as much as I did."

Girl, he was so egotistical. I didn't feel any enjoyment from him forcing himself on me. Then he said to me as he walked toward the door and as he opened it, "Clean yourself up now before Sam walks in and sees you like that, and don't you even think about saying anything to Sam or I'll say it was you who came on to me. I know you are mad right now, but soon you will come to believe we belong together."

I was still young minded and very naïve. I believed that men were capable of being kind and nice. I believed that some men could care about others rather than themselves. Sean's rape made me wonder if I was wrong. Were all men this way?

I stood there after he spoke those words. I had no clue what Sean would do after he made that statement to me, so after I finished cleaning up, I left before Sam or his mother came back. I couldn't look Sam or his mom in the face after what I just experienced with Sean. At that point, I felt Sean forced me to keep our horrible secret.

Eventually, it haunted me so much I decided to pray and ask God what I should do. That day after it happened, I went straight home. In my room, I fell on my knees and began to pray.

The next morning I heard the Lord as he spoke this scripture to my heart from the book of Proverbs 12:22 ESV: "Lying lips are an abomination to the Lord, but those who act faithfully are his delight."

Girl, I felt so much better knowing that I didn't have to hold on to his lie. Even if it hurt Sam, I knew telling the truth would set me free from the guilt and shame of what Sean did to me. I was happy that the Holy Spirit came to me that morning; it gave me the strength that I needed to tell Sam the truth.

After I arrived at school on Monday, I saw Sam between classes, and I asked, "Hi Sam, can we talk at lunch? Is that okay?"

"Sure, Babe, is everything okay at home?"

"Yes, everything is fine. So, I'll see you later?"

"Sure, Hon." He leaned over and gave me a kiss before he walked away.

Then, when we met for lunch, I asked if we could go out. He agreed, and once we got into his car, I said, "Sam, there's something I need to tell you about your brother. I don't know how you will take it, but I need to tell you anyway. When I was at your house last Saturday waiting for you to come home from football practice, I waited for you in your bedroom and Sean came in. He forced himself on me and raped me. When I tried to push him off of me, he became more aggressive."

Sam yelled, "What? He did this to you? Babe, this isn't your fault, it is my brother's. Sean has always been this way even when we were young kids. He tried talking to any girl that I started going out with just to prove to me he thinks he's better at knowing what a girl wants. I am really sorry that this happened to you.

It's my fault because I should have warned you about my brother. Please do not blame yourself, Babe. You did nothing wrong, and you sure didn't deserve what happened to you. If anyone should feel guilty here, it's me. I knew you were still a virgin just by how you acted around me, and I liked that about you. When you came to our high school, I noticed you right away. You weren't like the other girls who were all ready to give up their virginity to the football players. That is what drew me to you.

Babe, I don't want you to worry because I will tell our mom about this when I get home this evening. However, I'm not sure how your mother is going to take it that her daughter has been raped by Sam's big brother. Oh, I'm sure she will blame me for letting my brother do this to you. Either way, I don't want you to feel bad about what he did to you. This wasn't your fault, okay?"

"Okay, Sam. And I don't want you to worry about what my mom is going to think about you. And this wasn't your fault either because you are not your brother's keeper. This is all on Sean for doing this to me, and all so he can prove to himself that he's more of a man than you are."

At that point, Sam leaned over to give me a kiss. Once we both got back to the high school from lunch, we went to our last class for that day. After school, he went to football practice, and I went to soccer practice. I took the bus home because Sam was still at practice. And of course, when I got home, the first thing that I saw when I opened the door is my baby brother in the living room crawling towards me with a wet diaper.

Shortly after, I noticed my other three brothers running around outside. So I called them inside to see if they'd started their homework. At the same time, I changed my baby brother's diaper. No, my brothers hadn't even started their homework, so I made them sit at the table and do it.

Meanwhile, I began dinner for everyone, and then I went upstairs to knock on Mom's bedroom door. Her boyfriend, Eddie, answers, "What is it?"

I said, "Mom, I'm almost done with dinner, and the boys are doing their homework. Can you please give them a bath and put them to bed so that I can get my homework done before it gets later?"

She said, "Fine, I'll take care of it. Let me know when they finish eating, and I'll get the bath water ready."

"Mom, would it kill you to read them a bedtime story?"

"Why did you start doing that before bed? They are too tired to hear a bedtime story. Since you started the habit, why don't you do it, and then you can begin your homework."

"Yeah, Mom, and bedtime stories are a problem how?"

She said, "Okay, I see you find this funny, trying to guilt me into reading to my boys. I just never thought to do it. But why do you think I had you other than so that you can read to your brothers. I thought you said you had homework to do, and shouldn't you be doing that, Miss Thang?"

I wasn't ready to tell her about what happened to me yet. But, after a few weeks, I knew that I had a problem. I noticed I missed my menstrual period. At this point, I started freaking out. I stopped by the pharmacy to pick up a pregnancy test, and it turned out positive.

Now, Girl, I'm so angry because Sean stole my virginity and took away what Sam and I could have had together. Now everything was ruined, and I knew things would never be the same for us. In my head, I could hear my grandma saying, "God wants us to forgive those who curse us and those who hurt us," but at the same time, I wanted to be mad at Sean for what he did. Why should I forgive him after what he's done to me?

Here I was pregnant with his child, and I didn't love him. How could I look at this child and show it true love, knowing the truth about how it came into this world? My grandmother raised me, and she did not believe in abortion, so that wasn't an option for me.

Girl, that meant I had to carry Sean's baby inside me for nine months, and the thing that bothered me the most was that this wasn't Sam's child. My grandma used to say every child is God's miracle. She always had a way to make you feel peace from something as horrible as being raped. So, that night I prayed to ask God for his forgiveness for having these feelings toward this innocent child who did not ask to be here. I asked him to give me peace and the acceptance of this child that I now carried in my womb and to be a good mom to him or her.

6: THE LOST CHILD

The next morning God moved on my heart, from the book of John 14:27 NIV: "Peace I leave with you; my peace I give you. I do not give to you as the world gives. Do not let your hearts be troubled and do not be afraid." Wow! What such powerful words to hear from our God.

When I got to school, I saw Sam in the hall by the gym, and I said, "Hi, Sam, can we talk later?"

He said, "Sure, Babe, is everything okay?"

"Yes, and no."

"Okay, I can meet you in the cafeteria at 11:50 a.m." At lunch, Sam saw me sitting at the table by the window, and he walked over and said, "So what is this news you want to share with me?"

I answered, "Well, I'm pregnant."

"Wow! You're pregnant? I am not sure how to take this news, but mostly what do you want to do? Like I said, this is not your fault; it is my brother's. He is to blame, and I will make sure he steps up and help you if you decide to have it."

"Sam, abortion isn't an option in my family. I come from a religious family background, and having an abortion would be murder. It is a sin against God. But maybe I can put it up for adoption instead."

"Well, if you decide to bring this babe into the world, then my brother should do his part as the father. Whatever decision you make, I'm here to support that decision."

"I appreciate that so much, Sam," I said with relief. "But I have a couple of questions for you, though. First, do you think I should keep the baby? And second, do you believe your brother will truly be there for the babe?"

"Well, maybe this will change him from being such an asshole and help him grow up now that he might have someone else to think about other than himself."

"Okay, maybe you're right, and this babe perhaps will change him. Look, this is all overwhelming for me, and yes, I will tell Sean about the baby. Hell, I still haven't told my mom about what happened to me yet, and now that I am pregnant, I suppose I have to tell her soon. The only reason why I haven't told her is that she's been running behind her boyfriend Eddie these days."

"I want you to know that you are not alone here, especially after my brother forced himself on you. I'm thinking, why don't you come over tomorrow. We'll tell him together, and I'll make sure that our mom is there as well."

"Okay, that will be fine."

Sam stood up and said, "We need to get to our next class; I'll see you later, Babe." We hugged and gave each other a quick kiss then walked to our classes.

The next day was Saturday. I saw Mom asleep in her room, so I got dressed and left before she woke up.

Girl, if I didn't leave when I did, she'd tell me to make sure to feed my brothers and sisters. I was so sick and tired of being her maid and babysitter. It was high time for Mom to put her older daughter, Cookie, to work for a change; after all, she was the oldest. I was so tired of her getting away with doing nothing around the house!

Anyway, I went over to Sam's, and of course, Sean answered the door saying, "Well, good morning, Beautiful, I'm glad you're here. Sam told me that you were coming over today."

"I'm guessing that he told you why I was coming over today, right?"

At that moment, their mother walked into the living room and asked, "How are you, dear? Sam spoke with us about what Sean did, and I want you to know that I'm deeply sorry about everything, but we will get through this together, I promise."

"I'm doing great, Patricia, and thank you. Is Sam here?"

"Yes, he is dear; he'll be right down, and Sam also explained to me that your family doesn't believe in abortion. Well, I understand, and being that this wasn't your fault and believe you me, Sean will step up and take responsibility for this child."

"With my grandma being so religious, I know this would kill her if I got an abortion. As I learned from reading the Bible, according to the Book of Exodus 20:13 NIV: 'You shall not murder.'"

She answered, "I respect your grandma for teaching you about the Bible. They raised you right. I know some young women aren't ready to have children. And the way your mother treats you, she does not deserve to have a daughter like you."

As she finished her statement, I saw Sam walk into the living room, and he asked, "Well, did Mom explain to you that we spoke about Sean stepping up as a man?"

"Yes, she did. I'm happy to hear that I'm not going to be alone in this."

Sean came over to me and said, "First, I want you to know that I never meant to hurt you, and I am sorry for all of this. I will be there for you and the baby, and I won't make you do this alone. I will be responsible for what I've done to you. I want to be there when you start going to the prenatal care appointments if you let me."

I felt everything was going to be okay after Sam told his mom what Sean did; it wasn't as bad as I thought it would be. I guess praying about it helped.

Girl, Sam was such a kind and caring person; after all that happened, he still wanted to go out with me.

Sam said, "I know other people won't understand our situation, and you know what, I don't care whether or not people understand it. These are our lives, and this child is going to be loved. I want to be there with you even if it's my brother's baby. The fact is, I love you. Maybe for some strange reason, this could be a sign from God telling me it's time for me to stand up for myself and show my brother that I love you, and I'm not walking away from our relationship because of this."

"I love you too, Sam." I replied, "And you're right; no one has to know what your brother did to me." We both agreed not to tell anyone about this, but I had to tell my mom sooner than later. And, Girl, she's never gonna understand our situation.

I'm glad I'm sharing this with you, Girl, you're not judgmental like most people in the world. I feel it's not our job to judge others as long as God knows our secrets; that's all that matters to me.

I told Sam, "Not telling anyone will be the best thing for everyone, especially since this is a small town. Once the cat is out of the bag, everyone will know the truth."

"Yes, this is the way it should be, and things will work out for us in the long run."

Being a petite woman in my teens, I hid the pregnancy well. After my first prenatal doctor's appointment, we went to Sam's house. His mom was happy that things were going well for us, and the baby was doing great.

Sean was not happy that Sam and I still moved forward with our relationship. I had to forgive Sean for what he did to me, but that does not mean I will never forget it.

At the same time, I could hear my grandma in my head reminding me of the book of Ephesian 4:32 NIV: "Be kind and compassionate to one another, forgiving each other, just as in Christ God forgave you."

Girl, when you know what forgiveness is really all about, it makes it easy for you to let go. Forgiveness is about your salvation with God. When we don't forgive those who hurt us, it holds us back from experiencing God's true glory in life. I use to think that forgiveness was about the other person, which is why it took me such a long time to deeply understand what it meant.

I don't care what anyone says; I've found forgiveness to be challenging to accept in parts of my life. Whoever said life was going to be easy anyway, right, Girl? Life is about learning and experiencing what it has to offer. It's about being kind to one another. So you see, I truly had to let go of the pain that Sean inflicted on my life.

Girl, one of my biggest challenges was with trusting people. I've just told you about my bad childhood, experiencing evil with my stepdad, being kidnapped by a stranger, and now this with Sean. I often used to wonder as a child why God allowed this to happen to me. I began to think I attracted evil toward me. I always struggled with it in my mind, and I am sure I have more to experience in this world filled with cruelty, hatred, and envy, jealousy.

I started to resent God for blessing me with such an extremely bright light full of high vibration as a child; after a while, it felt more like a curse than a blessing. As I continued to learn more from the Bible, I realized my beauty wasn't a curse as I thought, but instead, it was a gift. My beauty wasn't just about my outside appearances; it was my goodness and kindness as well as my loving heart.

The next day during Sunday school, our lesson was on Genesis chapter 12: verses 11-12. Abram was terrified by the beauty of his wife, Sarai. Before they entered Egypt, he asked his wife to lie and say that she was his sister to stay alive. Otherwise, they would have killed him and let her stay alive. From that moment on, I learned to appreciate my gift.

So, Girl, as things continued to work out for Sam and me, Sean started to become more controlling. I believe this was because Sam and I were still together, and Sean was beginning to feel left out of everything, including going to the prenatal appointments.

Sean came into the bedroom where Sam and I were watching a movie and said, "Sam, what the hell is going on here? Are you two having sex while she is carrying my child? And if you are, is that even safe for the baby?"

Sam huffed, "First off, Sean, no, we are not having sex. Secondly, it is none of your business what we do, so you need to back off here, bro. Just because you impregnated her doesn't give you the right to control her or what she does with her body, Sean."

This situation was becoming stressful. Whenever Sam and I got together on the weekend, Sean would intentionally come into Sam's room to interrupt us. Most of the time, we were just watching a movie. I saw Sean coming between Sam and me, and, Girl, it started to feel like Sean was holding me hostage just because I was carrying his child.

Sean didn't care if I loved him or not; it was about keeping me from Sam. Sean made it very clear to me that as long as I carried his child, Sam would never touch me. It was obvious that he wanted to come between our relationship.

Sam was such a kind person; he saw the stress this was causing me, and he didn't want to see me suffer. Sean was never going to let Sam play daddy to his child. The last time Sean came into Sam's room, he was being an asshole to Sam, which is why I believe Sam and I broke off our relationship.

At school the next day, Sam said, "Look, I know what we have is so amazing but let's face it as long as we stay together, my brother is going to always be around giving the two of us hell, and you know that isn't good for the baby. And I know you feel the same way that I do."

I answered, "Of course I do, but who's to say that he will keep making things hard for us? Maybe he will start to see how strong our love is for each other, right? If we don't give in to him, he will stop causing a problem for us."

"I wish that would be the case, but I know my brother, he's always been envious of me since we were kids. He always felt that Mom and Dad loved me more than him for some reason. I am really sorry that our relationship has to end like this, but I believe it's the right thing to do for the sake of the baby. I hope we can still be friends. We have so much love between us; I don't want to lose that part of our relationship. I'm willing to be there for you."

THE LOST CHILD

Girl, I agreed because I loved him enough to let him go. Plus, Sam was such a great guy.

I continued going to my prenatal care appointments alone, but Sean showed up at the clinic one day. He asked, "Is it okay if I start coming with you to the doctor's appointments? Since I'm the father of our child, it should be me instead of Sam, is all I'm saying here."

Even though I was mad at him, he was starting to show another side of himself when he talked about the baby and me. Then I thought maybe he was acting kinder to me because he knew Sam and I weren't together anymore. I guess he figured he had full control over things now that his brother was out of the picture.

Of course, at that time, I was not aware that pregnancy causes your sexual hormones to get out of control. Let's just say I was starting to crave sex, and Sean happened to be in the right place at the right time. Right, Girl?

After the appointment, Sean says, "I need to run by the house for a minute to grab something for band practice this evening." As he pulled up to the house, he asked if I had to use the bathroom, and of course, I did. So when we entered the house, Sean said, "You can use the bathroom down the hall on the right." Which was, by the way, next to his bedroom. And yes, you guessed it, Girl.

As I came out of the bathroom, Sean came up to me and began touching my breasts, which he'd noticed getting bigger due to the pregnancy. At that point, because of the hormones, I started to enjoy it.

Girl, from there he took me in his bedroom, and said, "I've been reading about how being pregnant makes pregnant women horny, is it true, and are you right now?"

Hmm. "Yes, I am right now, but I thought you told Sam that it wasn't good for the baby. So are you saying that it is?"

"I know what I said, but I admit I was wrong. After reading up on pregnancy, I learned how it makes hormones, and ladies become very sexual."

"Oh, I see, it never ceases to amaze me that the only thing that stands out to you is the woman's hormones. Did you read where it states if it's good for the baby?" Of course, he was speechless because he was too preoccupied.

After that day, Sean and I started to have a lot of sex, and the next thing I knew, I fell in love with him. Girl, I know what you are thinking, why would I fall for Sean after what he has done, right? I was young, and it's too complicated to try and figure out the hormones and the feelings pouring out of me.

Anyway, time passed. My uncle had a band, and he came over to Mom's house to visit, and he asked me if I want to fill in for him as the lead female singer. His lead female vocalist was out sick, and he needed someone to step in until she gets back.

Girl, I was so excited to do it one because I love music. I went to a couple of rehearsals before the first set. The biggest problem was my young age and how my uncle was going to get me in the club. Then, that day on my break, I notice that Sean's band was playing that weekend too.

This old hotel building was under construction, and the owner rented out a few of the rooms to the band members. A few of us took our break at the same time as Sean's band members.

Girl, that's when I stumbled across the noise of people having sex. Of course, I felt as if something was pulling me towards the sound. As I got closer to the sound, I could see into the corner of the suite. I saw Sean thrusting behind a woman.

After seeing Sean having sex with that woman, Girl, you can imagine how I felt. My feelings at that split second were mixed. The first feeling coming at me was betrayal and hurt. But once I got far away from that hotel room, I ended up in another empty room with only a couch and chair and a few tables. I said to myself, "Connie, get a grip. You knew that Sean was a wild one from what Sam told you."

So why was I lying there crying my eyes out? It was because of all the hormones going through my body. I eventually fell asleep on the couch, worn out by the tears. I lost track of time, and by the time I woke up, it was 6:45 the next morning. I was sure my uncle was worried about me, and of course, as I walked down the hall, I heard Uncle Jeff calling me. I turned the corner, and I saw Clyde with him as well.

I said, "I'm right here, and I'm okay. I saw Sean with another woman last night on my break, and I ran off into one of the empty rooms and fell asleep from crying. But I'm okay now."

Uncle Jeff said, "Well, my niece, you can't get yourself involved with any band members, especially drummers. They tend to sleep with every woman in a skirt. I'm sorry that you had to experience that. At the same time, it's all a part of falling in love."

Clyde said, "Your mom told me to come to find you because she was worried."

I replied, "So you're my mom's watchdog now? I'm fine, and I can take care of myself, Clyde. I don't need her to send you to check up on me whenever she needs me to take care of my siblings for her."

Uncle Jeff said, "You know that your mom loves you. She just has a funny kind of way of showing it to you."

Girl, Clyde grew up with my uncle's, and I saw him at my mom's fish-fry on Friday evenings. Clyde said, "I'm not leaving until you come with me. I told your mom that I wouldn't come back without you, so you may as well come."

I went with them. On the drive home, I sat in the back seat and thought to myself, "I'm so done with Sean. I will not let him hurt me anymore because it has become clear that he wasn't serious about being with me. As far as the baby goes, he's the father of my baby, nothing more."

I was so angry at myself for getting all wrapped up with Sean in the first place.

Girl, now I've got no one to talk to and to get me through this pregnancy. As far as my hormones go? I'm a pregnant woman left with all these horny hormones and no one to help me through them. Now, what am I gonna do here with all these hormones?

I did find one friend to talk with and asked her, "I am sure you experienced this when you carried your twins, right?"

She said, "Oh, yes, I did! It was hell. My breasts were tender all the time, and I stayed horny up until my thirty-second week."

"What? Do you mean to tell me that this is what I'm looking forward to through my whole pregnancy? Oh my!"

Girl, I still haven't told my mom that I was pregnant yet, and she certainly doesn't know that it was because of Sean raping me. I don't think that I'll tell her that part either. Other than you, Girl, Clyde is the only one that knows I was raped, other than Sam and his mom.

One night when Clyde was at our house watching a movie, I told him about the rape and told him I hadn't told Mom. He said to me that was between me and my mom. He told me he wouldn't say anything.

On top of all this, I was still trying to figure out if I was going to move out of Mom's house and get my own place before the baby comes.

On the next school day, I couldn't believe it; Sean came up to the high school, and when he saw me walking down the hall, he came over to me, asking, "Can we talk please?"

I said, "Sean, why are you here? I do not want to talk to you because we have nothing to talk about. It was very clear after seeing you last weekend with that woman you aren't ready to play house with me. And there's no need to tell me that you're sorry, just to make me feel better or what you believe I want to hear. You don't have to worry. I'm not saying that you can't be a father to our child. But what I am trying to say is, there's no more of us, Sean."

"Look, I made a mistake. I was drunk, and she came on to me after we finished our gig. Honey, it's the truth. I really do love you, and all I'm asking here is, please give me another chance. I want to prove to you that I am ready to be there for you and the baby."

Girl, I was powerless once he began singing that sweet tune. Truth be told, I was a sucker when it came to trusting men, even after catching him in the act. Maybe because I was programmed to forgive those who hurt you, or maybe it is as simple as wanting to have a healthy family of my own. Was that asking too much?

We began walking toward the school exit and into the parking lot. He asked if he could take me home, and I said yes.

Girl, I often wonder if our life lessons are a part of God's plan for our lives. Now, I was starting to believe that maybe my agony and suffering from my mom's neglect as a child made me grow much faster than an average child. And raising my sibling was part of pushing me toward my destiny. So that one day, I would become a great mom and an awesome wife. We all deserve to have that in our lives. I mean right, don't you agree? I am a sucker for happiness. It's what every woman wants.

Just as I got into the house, I saw mom there without her boyfriend. Now was the only chance I'd have to tell her that I was pregnant. As I closed the door behind me, she told me, "I need you to cook this evening because I have something to do right now. You look like you want to talk to me about something that happened at the school. The school can call me, but we'll talk when I get back."

Right after she said that she went straight upstairs to her bedroom to get dressed and meet her boyfriend uptown, I'm thinking she went to get more drugs.

As weeks go by, Sean and I started spending time together. Shockingly things were going very well until one Monday morning when I got to school late. I had to stop by the office to get a late pass to go to class. Outside the office was a table where another student was signing people up for a political debate. After getting my pass, I left the office, and just then, a group of the football players came charging down the hall.

These football players arrived in front of the office playing around, pushing and shoving. The next thing I know, a corner of the debate sign-up table was accidentally thrust into my stomach.

And, Girl, immediately after, the football players realized what happened. But it was much too late at that point. They apologized to me and the other student.

I saw Sam walking quickly toward the crowd, worry covering his face. No one knew that I was pregnant, but Sam. He started yelling at the football players, "What the hell were you guys thinking here? Don't you know people can get hurt with you guys playing around in front of the office like that? Come on, guys, really that was super stupid."

I went to the nurse's office, told her that I experienced stomach pain, and asked if I could leave for the day. She said yes and gave me a written note to give to the front desk. The office would let the rest of my teachers know that I was leaving because I did not feel good.

When I got home, I started bleeding. I bled all the way into that evening, and Girl, the pain was so freaking awful.

Clyde, who was over visiting, asked, "Are you okay?"

"No, I'm not. Something happened at school today, and I need to go to the hospital, like right now."

"Okay, let's tell your mom that I'm taking you to the hospital and see if she wants to come."

As he started to go upstairs, Mom was coming down, so she said, "What! Why are you taking her to the hospital, Clyde?"

That's when I replied, "Mom, because I'm pregnant and something is wrong. I started bleeding. Now, can we go already?"

When we arrived at the hospital, the nurse at the desk asked me a few questions "Can you tell me what's going on here, my dear?"

I told her what happened at high school that day, and that I was sixteen weeks pregnant. I also told her that when I got home, I started experiencing bleeding from the incident. As she continued with her questions, the pain started increasing, and, Girl, I was in so much pain I just couldn't answer any more questions because of it.

My mom started yelling at the nurse, "Look, lady, can't you see my daughter is in pain, and she's bleeding really bad. So this is not the time for you to continue with these ridiculous questions, can't you see she's pregnant? I'm sure you are just trying to do your job, but now is not the time. You need to give her something to stop the pain, don't you think?"

That's when the nurse stated, "The doctor is going to want to see her before I can give your daughter something for her pain. He will want to run a few tests to make sure everything looks okay."

After the nurse took my blood, she said, "The doctor will be in shortly once we get the blood work back."

Mom replied, "In the meantime, is there anything you can give her to ease the pain until the test comes back?"

"No, but don't worry, the doctor will be in right away once the test is back from the lab."

When the doctor came into the room, he started touching my stomach area, asking me if this hurt. Through clenched teeth, I growled, "Yes! It hurts like hell!"

Calmly he said to me, "Well, my dear, you're having a miscarriage. I'm sure that you are experiencing severe pain because of it. But don't worry, after we do a DNC on you and remove the fetus from your uterus, I'll prescribe some pain medication for you to take at home. After a week, you'll begin feeling better."

Then the nurse came in, and the doctor told her what he needed her to prepare for the procedure. He turned to me, saying, "You just relax. We'll have you done soon, and you'll be released once everything is done."

Girl, part of me felt so relieved just to have the pain go away, yet on the other hand, I was sad to lose the baby. I believe God was giving me another chance at finding true love one day.

When the doctor and the nurse came back in the hospital room, they did the procedure and released me after thirty minutes. When I got home, I called Sean to explain what happened. Girl, I could tell that he was sad after I finished telling him, and I heard him breathing, but he didn't say a word for a few seconds. Then he finally found the words to say, "I'm really sorry that this happened to you, Babe. Are you ok?"

"Yes, I'm doing fine, but are you okay? After all, it was your baby too."

"I was looking forward to raising our child together. I know this will change things between us now, but I hope not because I really do I love you."

"Yes, this will change things for us, Sean. The only reason we were together is because of the baby; this wasn't the way I pictured falling in love with someone, and you almost took that from me. Now I can still dream of having that experience. But, I do wish you the best, Sean, goodbye." I do believe God saw my heart and how things would have been if I'd had the baby by Sean.

That night after falling asleep, God spoke to me the Holy word from the book of Isaiah 41:10 NIV: "So do not fear, for I am with you; do not be dismayed, for I am your God. I will strengthen you and help you; I will uphold you with my righteous right hand."

When we carefully listen to our intuition and our inner higher-self, it is God's way of trying to guide us to the true life we deserve. When we get that gut feeling in the pit of our stomach, that's when we should trust it.

And so, I knew it was not meant for me to have that baby, and God gave me peace of mind. As the months passed, Sam and I just became friends in the end. We both had been through enough drama, dealing with his brother and my family, and decided being friends was easier and more comforting.

7: MOVING OUT

One day Mom came into my bedroom and told me that I was going on birth control pills. I said, "Mom, you are a little too late to give me some advice on that; I've already scheduled an appointment with the clinic. Perhaps you should be thinking about going on the pill yourself."
 The next thing I knew, she slapped me across my face. "Mom, really? All I have to do is call Grandma and Grandpa, and they'll come over and pick me up. Then who will you have around here to be your live-in nanny?"
 "You'll call them over my dead body. Not if I have something to say about it."
 Girl, as she turned to walk out of my room, I heard her mumbling, "The only way she'll get out of this house is when hell freezes over. Who the hell does she think she is around here? Fast-ass heifer!"
 I was so done with taking care of my younger siblings. While she continued to go out with her man, Eddie, to drink and do drugs, I was here doing her job. I'm not saying that I didn't love my sisters and brothers, but I'd had enough!
 That weekend Clyde hung out around the house like a lost puppy. I'm sure he was hoping that I'd give him a chance, but no, I was not into him like that.
 I know God gave me another chance to find true love, but how was that going to happen while I lived with my mom? Meanwhile, I wanted to finish high school, which meant I had two more years before graduation.
 After about nine months go by, one night on the weekend, I was watching a movie, and Clyde was there as well. Girl, you remember when Clyde came looking for me

that time I caught Sean with another woman? I felt he must care for me enough to do what my mom told him, right? Since that day, he has always been around to help me with my siblings whenever Mom would take off with the food stamps and sell them for drug money.

This thought crossed my mind, "Hmmm, what if I get Clyde to get me pregnant?" I think at that point I just wanted out of my mom's house so badly. Getting pregnant from Clyde was the best idea I could come up with.

Clyde wasn't my ideal man if I felt I had a choice, but he had a job, and I saw that he was a responsible human being according to what my naked eyes could see. Maybe if I got pregnant, it would be a way I could move out of Mom's house and get my own place with no strings attached, hmmm.

I am just saying, Girl, getting pregnant may not be the best idea that I came up with, but it was either that or put up with my mom for two more years as she did drugs and pushed her responsibility on me. All I wanted to do was get a place for myself, which meant I really had to focus on finishing high school.

After thinking about this exit plan for a while, I warmed to it. One night I was downstairs on the couch watching TV, and Clyde started coming on to me.

The next thing I knew, we were having sex, and of course, a month later, I was pregnant. Girl, at that point, I didn't care because I was determined to get out of my mom's house.

Even though I wasn't in love with Clyde, it could all work out for both of us. He'd have someone at home who would cook and take care of him.

I thought this plan would be good enough until God brought him someone who would truly love him. All I knew was that I wasn't the one to love him, but this was a way out of the hell that I was living in.

Girl, I was so happy to say goodbye to Mom, and hello to the beginning of this new chapter in my life. I knew being free from her abuse was going to be hard at first, but it would start getting easier down the road. I knew that I could work and take care of my baby. How hard would it be, right? I took care of my siblings, right?

As soon as my mom found out that I was pregnant, and by whom, part of her was relieved, but she kicked me out of her house anyway. I couldn't understand why she pretended to be mad when she was the one who was pushing him on me from the beginning.

Clyde was there that morning, and he asked if I wanted to stay with his sister Geraldine and I said to him, "Yes, any place but here would be better. And, just so we're clear, living with your sister is only short term, right? because I know we're planning on finding our own place eventually."

He said, "I know you want our own place, and I'll start working on that."

Girl, when I met his sister for the first time, she seemed like a nice and happy person. She warmly welcomed me into her home. Clyde and I started saving our money to get our own place one day.

Once things began to get settled, I started working part-time during school. The high school had a program for students who wanted to earn extra credit while attending school.

I worked for a middle-aged Caucasian man who had a lot of businesses around town. I started working at one of his construction sites.

He noticed that I was pregnant, so he trained me as a receptionist to answer the phones and file the contracts. It wasn't the greatest opportunity, but it allowed me the chance to graduate early from high school. Things were looking good until the school got the news that I was pregnant.

They told me that I couldn't attend high school because of my pregnancy, and they registered me into a G.E.D. program where they put pregnant teenage girls my age. I continued my evening classes to get my diploma, and I

MOVING OUT

was still able to work in the extra credit program, as long as I was attending my evening classes.

It was so nice to be able to work and keep my own money for a change! I began saving it for my place. My boss, Mr. Charles, noticed that I worked hard at my job, and he asked me if I wanted more hours. He said if I wanted to, I could work on the weekends. I told him I'd love more hours, so we agreed on it with big smiles on our faces.

He was the nicest white man I ever met in Southern Illinois. Before I knew it, time began to fly, like it always does when you're not expecting it to. I finally had my daughter, and we found a place to live in a trailer home, which wasn't far from my high school. Back then, the rent was reasonable for a two-bedroom for me and my daughter. Clyde's job took him out of town for a couple of weeks at a time, but he stayed with us when he was in town.

Girl, after six months, I went over to Mom's to visit my siblings. I knew they wanted to see their niece. When I got there, my older sister said she would babysit her for me while I went to the grocery store.

Cookie decided to take my baby out to the park, just so she could show her off to her friends, but she forgot to take her blanket to cover her, and that evening my baby was colicky.

It was late when I returned from the store, so I decided to just stay at Mom's house. My baby cried all night, and Girl, I had no idea what to do to get her to stop crying. My mom had no clue, either. That's when I called my grandma to ask her what to do, and she told me to blow cigarette smoke on the top of her soft spot on her head. Who knew blowing cigarette smoke on a baby's soft spot would quiet them down? My grandma had many more of these crazy homemade home remedies.

As soon as I got her to sleep, my mom's asshole boyfriend kept coming in and out of the room where we were trying to sleep. That's when I got up and went into

Mom's room, "Can you please tell your creepy boyfriend to stop coming in the girls' room? Every time he opens and closes the door, he wakes up the baby."

As I stood in Mom's doorway, he put his hand in my face and said, "Look, little girl, if you only knew what kind of man I really am, you wouldn't talk to me this way. I've murdered women for far less, so if I were you, I would stay in a child's place."

Girl, my mom was so high she said nothing to him after he said that to me, and the next day I called Clyde to tell him about it. While I talked with Clyde, I put my things into my car to drive home. Clyde asked, "He said what? Where is he now?"

"In Mom's room, I guess. I'm on my way home in a few minutes, because you can only put up with so much whenever you're here at Mom's place."

"I'll speak to Ruby sometime this week when I get back into town. Meanwhile, you just stay away from this man because I don't want to end up going to jail by hurting him if he puts his hands on you. Especially when he disrespects you when all you were asking from him is to stop opening open and closing the door."

"Mom doesn't care about anything but getting high. All she said to him was, 'Eddie, come on leave her alone so she can go back to the baby to get her to sleep again.'"

Girl, after I got off the phone with Clyde, I left and went to my trailer home. Later that week, when Clyde came home, he told me that he was going over to Mom's this weekend to talk to her about Eddie. I'm not going to lie here; I was very happy to hear that he'd stop by there to talk to Mom about Eddie threatening me. Who knew what he was capable of. We didn't know this man, and I'm sure my mom didn't either.

After dinner, I said to Clyde, "I really appreciate that you want to stand up for me the way you do. No one other than my grandparents and my uncles ever stood up for me in my whole life. I know you are the father to our child, but I want to be honest with you, Clyde, and please don't take this the wrong way. I'm not in love with you the way that you are with me, which is why I want to be open and honest with you about my feelings toward you."

"I'm happy to stand up for you when it comes down to it with my family." He paused, then continued, "What are your feelings for me?"

"It's like a really good friend kind of feelings, and I don't want you to be hurt by me being honest about my feelings towards you. If you can't handle it, then I will definitely understand if you don't want to live together."

"I understand. All I want is to be there for you and my daughter, and if nothing else, at least I will feel better knowing that the two of you are safe. Even if you don't love me in that way at this point, I really do care about you."

The next day, while we were both at work, his sister looked after our daughter. Girl, this crazy man Eddie found out where we lived. He went over to our trailer, broke in, and took the refrigerator out of the trailer.

When I arrived home that early evening, I noticed that the fridge was gone. I picked up the phone and called the landlord to see if he stopped by and took it to have it serviced or something. I thought that would be odd because I didn't recall having any problem with it, but who the hell knows, at this point.

When he answered, I said, "Hi Bill, this is Connie. Was there something wrong with the refrigerator?"

"Of course not, why?"

"Well, it's not here in my trailer, and the door was unlocked, which was weird. That's when I decided to give you a call. I thought maybe you came over to repair it or something."

"I always give a twenty-four-hour notice before coming into the tenant trailer. Just give me a minute; I'll be right over."

Girl, when I first met this man, he was flirty with me, and I wasn't comfortable with him coming over when Clyde wasn't there. But in this case, I had no choice.

When he arrived, he began accusing me of lying and selling his refrigerator.

Soon after, he started making sexual advances to me, reaching out to touch my shoulders, feeling my breasts, saying, "You know, I can forget about this if you give me what I want; that is by letting me kiss your body, especially between your legs."

Girl, how disgusting! I pushed him off me, and I grabbed the first thing that I saw, which was the hammer on the counter. Seeing that, he moved away from the door, and I ran out and down to my neighbor's trailer. When she opened her front door, she cried out, "What's wrong?"

I told her what happened, and she said, "You should call the police on this man because he had no right to touch you in that way; that's sexual-harassment for him to do that to a woman and especially his tenant."

As soon as she began dialing the 911, I noticed the police lights outside. We both went out to explain what happened to the police, but the officer asked me to walk back to my trailer with him to get my side of the story. When we opened my door, I noticed the landlord was standing over by the other police vehicle. The officer turned with the notepad and pen in his hand as he began taking notes.

He asked, "Did you threaten the landlord with a hammer?"

"Yes, but I can explain why I did, officer."

"Okay, why don't you explain to me what took place here."

"What happened is my landlord started touching me on my breasts and saying that I have to pay him back with sex for selling his refrigerator. And the thing is, officer, it was my mom's boyfriend who stole the refrigerator."

The police officer asked, "Ma'am, is this true?"

"Yes! That's when I picked up the phone and called him, and he came over and started accusing me of selling it. Then, he began touching me inappropriately, which is when I grabbed the hammer and asked him to leave my trailer. But he wouldn't, that is when I ran out of my trailer and to the neighbor's to call you guys. But I saw that you were already here, and that's when I came out to explain my story to you."

Oh no, now Girl, because I'm an African American woman and he is a white man, they arrested me that evening. I thought to myself, "What the fuck? Here I am in the back seat of a cop car. Just for reporting someone else's bad deed."

Girl, wouldn't you agree with me if this happened to a white woman, do you think she would have been arrested for trying to protect herself? No, I don't believe that would happen.

When Clyde got home, the neighbor woman went down to our trailer and told him what happened. The next day, he took off from work so he could go to the jail to see how much my bail was and to try to get me out. When he got there, they said my bail was $5,000. They let me speak with Clyde, and that's when I explained to him what happened.

He said, "I will call a bailsman to get you out. Just hold tight for me, okay?"

"I need you to call my boss, Mr. Charles, so he knows what is going on. Just tell him what happened, so he won't think I'm skipping work today, okay?"

Within hours, Clyde got me out. When I got to work, I explained the situation to my boss. To my surprise, he said, "Listen, I can try to speak to the prosecutor and the judge to see about getting the charges dropped, or maybe have the charges dropped to a gross misdemeanor because you did nothing wrong here other than trying to defend yourself against your landlord who came into your trailer and tried to force you, via sexual favors, to pay him back for the stolen refrigerator. That in itself should be a crime against him for coming on to a young teenager. I don't understand the justice system at all these days.

"I'll get a private investigator to look into Eddie's background, and whatever they might find, I will give it to the prosecutor's office to use against him. Do you know Eddie's full name?"

"No, but I can get it from my mom when I see her this week."

"Okay, you start working on that. Meanwhile, I'll give your landlord a call as well because he had no right to come at you that way. It's sexual harassment toward his tenant. Maybe I can get him to reconsider his police statement."

Girl, if it wasn't for Mr. Charles being there for me in court, who knows what the judge and the prosecutor may have done in my case. That next week in court, the judge asked me if I knew who stole the refrigerator.

"Yes, your honor, I do."

The judge then said, "Well, after speaking with Mr. Charles, I have information that explains things more clearly. Therefore, I propose reducing the charge to a gross misdemeanor instead of an assault."

I walked out of the courtroom, so happy. When we got home, I said, "Clyde, I don't want to live here anymore because this landlord is so creepy, and I don't trust him at all, especially not after what he did."

Clyde said, "Then we'll look for another place to live. Meanwhile, we can stay with my sister again until we do find something."

"Okay, that sounds good." That weekend, we packed up all our stuff and placed it in storage. His sister was glad to help us because it meant she could spend time with and spoil her niece. I finally had a chance to catch up on my sleep that weekend.

It was also good to hear her get onto Clyde about his drinking. She said things like, "Maybe you shouldn't be in the street as much hanging out with your friends since you have a daughter to think about now. You've got to think about more than yourself. Why do you have to hang out with them all the time? Is it so you'll work on their cars? That's the time you need to be spending with Connie and your daughter."

She was right. But even though he was doing that, I didn't care because he and I weren't really together like a couple anyway. But his sister didn't know our arrangement, and we didn't tell her.

After living with his sister for a while, we found another place. We moved in and unpacked.

8: SAVED BY GOD'S ANGEL

Everything was going okay with us until a year goes by, and I get pregnant again. Little things were starting to bother me. The back yard and driveway were covered with black oil from Clyde's side gig fixing cars, and our sex life didn't provide any enjoyment for me.

I wanted more for my life than being with someone just because we shared children together. We didn't have anything in common other than our children. I just wasn't happy anymore with our arrangement, and I felt I was wasting my life away.

Girl, I ended up moving back in with my mom since Eddie wasn't there anymore. My daughter was a year old, and my son was a few months old.

My older sister, Cookie, and a friend of the family, Betty, wanted to go out, and they asked if I wanted to be their designated driver for the night. I figured why not since I generally didn't drink, and only occasionally smoked a little marijuana—I was more of a lightweight when it came to partying.

I saw Mom coming down the stairs, and she said, "Well, I'll help watch the kids as long as you guys come straight back home after the bar. Is that a deal?"

We all agreed as we walked out the door. However, as soon as we got to the club, Betty said, "Oh, my guy is here!"

I asked, "How long have you known this guy, Betty?"

"I met him the last time he was here. He and his friend are okay, girl."

"Betty, I did not come to the bar to pick up guys." Cookie and Betty told me to speak for myself because they were there looking. We all went into the club, and I split off.

I was dancing and having a great time until Betty came over to me, asking, "Girl, can you go outside with me to get some air? It's hot in here."

When we got outside, I saw two guys sitting in their car, and she tells me, "I know what you are about to say, but come on, Connie. Just take a ride with us. I'm sure they are just going around the block to smoke some weed, and I'm sure you want some, right? Oh, come on, please."

At that point, I got in the back, and Betty got in the front seat. She began flirting with the driver, and after they finish smoking the weed, we drove back toward the club. Instead of stopping, we passed right by the club.

At that point, I was getting uncomfortable and spoke up, "Betty, where the hell are they taking us? I never agreed to this. You never said anything about going anywhere other than drive around to finish smoking the joint. Please take me back to the club, dude."

"I know I said that." Then she turns to ask the driver, "You never said that we were going anywhere, so where are you taking us?"

Girl, that's when the guy next to me said, "Is there something wrong with taking a drive away from the club? It is not like we are going to do anything to you, ladies. We don't want to draw attention to ourselves because of the marijuana; it makes us look suspicious. We don't want to get arrested by cops. You just need to relax; we'll bring you guys back after we finish smoking this joint. Is that okay with you, Miss Lady?"

I replied, "It would have been nice to know this before driving off from the club. It would have given me a chance to agree to go with you guys or not. No, this is not okay."

Eventually, they pulled up to a house in the Lake Height's area, and I wondered who they knew that lived there. Girl, I had no idea that it was going to turn into a crazy nightmare. After arriving at a house where neither

Betty nor I knew anyone, the driver said, "I just need to run inside for a minute, but it won't take me long."

The other guy said, "Come in for a minute; I have to use the toilet."

Girl, I got a bad feeling in the pit of my stomach after he suggested we come in. My intuition told me that this guy from the back seat was bad news. As soon as we got inside, the driver said, "Oh, shit. I thought I had cigarettes here, but I don't, so I'll have to go out and buy some. But no worries, we'll be right back." I felt the fear of terror blow into my heart.

I stood up from the kitchen table and said, "What the hell is going on here, Betty? I'm not going to stay here with this guy I don't know. What the fuck? I'm going with you guys, and you can drop me off at the club while you are at it."

The driver said, "Come on, my friend doesn't bite. You'll be okay until we get back."

"I don't give a rat ass if he does bite. I didn't agree to be here on a blind set up, and I don't appreciate being pushed into this, so take me back to the club now."

That is when the guy from the backseat came out of the bathroom and over to me, saying, "You are one stuck up bitch."

"Bitch? I'm not your bitch, and I am not the one who lied to get me to come along with you. Are you that desperate to get hooked-up that you pretend to ride around to smoke a joint and then bring us here? Dude, that's lame. You need to brush up on your game, and if you think you're going to fuck me? Oh man, you are about to get a rude awakening call."

He whined, "Come on, I'm not going to do anything to you. Why can't you just loosen up a little and come sit in the living room? You don't even have to sit by me."

"Why would I do that when I'm about to leave in a few minutes?"

"They'll be back in five minutes."

"When they get back, he's going to take me back to the club because I have to drive my sister back home after the club closes."

"Why can't she drive herself back home from the club? Why does she need you to drive her?"

"Because she wanted to drink and have fun."

"I'll take you when my friend comes back, but only if you come and sit down in the living room. I promise I won't do anything to you if you don't want me to."

"I don't want to sit in there. I'm okay right here in the kitchen."

Girl, that night, my guardian angel watched over me. After the dude from the back seat stated again that he would take me back to the club when his friend gets back, I went into the living room and sat on the opposite end of the couch from him.

About fifteen seconds later, he began getting aggressive with me, to the point we were physically wrestling. I started praying silently, and right before he started pulling my pants down, I heard a soft whisper in my right ear saying, "You have to use the bathroom."

I said to him very loudly, "I have to use the bathroom."

He replied, "Girl if you are lying to me, I'm going to beat the hell out of you. Do you hear me bitch?"

"I'm not lying. I have to use the bathroom."

"Okay, go."

Oh my God, Girl, my heart was beating so fast! Once I got to the bathroom, I locked the door immediately. I was so scared.

After twenty minutes go by, this guy starts beating on the bathroom door, saying, "Bitch, open this door. If you don't, I'll kick this damn door down and kill you. Do you hear me bitch?"

I started praying, "God, please don't let him get in here. Forgive me for any sin that I may have missed when praying at night in Jesus's name, amen."

The next thing I knew, I heard the birds singing outside the bathroom window. I looked up and saw the sun shining in. I felt the protection of God that whole night; then I heard a soft voice again whispering to me, "Now is the time for you to open the door and leave."

Girl, at this point, I wasn't going to stop trusting in the angels now. I opened the door. I walked out of the bathroom and saw the guy asleep on the living room floor by the couch. I turned and went back towards the other rooms to see if Betty was in one of them. Sure enough, she was in the last room down the hall, laying naked with her legs across her guy's body.

I woke her ass up, whispering, "Betty, get up and let's go before the other guy wakes up. Last night, after you guys left to supposedly get some cigarettes, he tried to rape me."

She said, "Oh, my God! Can you help me find my glasses so we can get out of here? I can't see without them. I'm so sorry, Connie."

I quietly started looking around, so I didn't wake the guy up; that would be the last thing I needed. Eventually, I looked under the second bed, and that's where they were. I crawled under the bed to retrieve them and gave them to her while she dressed. We quietly began walking toward the front door, and when we got outside, the two of us ran as fast as we could until we got to the end of the road.

Betty says, "I'm going to walk home since I'm not too far from my house, are you going to be alright?"

"Yes, I'll be fine." Girl, I was so freaking mad at Betty at this point, not to mention she only had a few blocks to go before she made it home. I had to walk five blocks to pick up my car at the club.

When I got home, Mom said, "So, did you forget the agreement we made, or what?"

"No, Mom, I didn't forget. Betty's drunk-ass, put me in a bad situation last night when she asked me to sit in the car with these two guys who were from St. Louis. They ended up taking us to some house in Lake Heights. Then she and the driver left me with his friend, who tried to rape me. And, Mom, the angels knew what might happen to me, and I heard the angels speak to me. They told me to go and lock myself in the bathroom, where I stayed all night until they gave me a sign in the morning. By the grace of God, this guy fell asleep, and was sleeping until I got out of there this morning." Then I asked her, "Did Cookie make it home last night?"

"Yeah, she made it here okay. She's upstairs in bed; I'm sure with a hangover."

"Where's the kids?"

"They both are upstairs in my bed, sleeping too."

Then, of course, Clyde comes walking in the front door, asking, "Can I see our kids? That's why I came by this morning."

"They're asleep upstairs in Mom's room."

Then Clyde asked, "Where did you go last night? I know that you wasn't here because I came by, and Ruby said you went out with the girls."

"Yes, Cookie asked if I would be their designated driver, but later that night, I had to fight off some crazy-ass guy who tried to rape me. I owe it all to drunk-ass Betty. She told me that she knew these guys, and then she asked if I would go outside with her. We ended up in Lake Heights. Then her dumb-ass left me with this guy. To stay safe, I ended up locked in the bathroom all night until morning."

"What the hell! Are you serious? Why did you agree to be her designated driver in the first place?"

"Oh, my God, I'm too tired to stand here explaining to you what I've been through all night. I have the angels looking after me now, and I don't need you to be all over me for deciding to drive my sister and Betty to the club. I was trying to be nice, and I thought it might be fun to get out a little, but I had no idea that Betty was going to put me in a bad situation."

"Well, you don't need to take her to the club anymore because she is a crazy old drunk who only cares about herself."

9: NEW CITY

Girl, all my life, I've been around my mom and her friends who are alcoholics and drug users, and I'm so tired of being around people that can't handle their alcohol. And according to the Book of 1 Peter 5:8 ESV: "Be sober-minded; be watchful. Your adversary, the devil, prowls around like a roaring lion, seeking someone to devour."

You always have to be careful and always trust your intuition, especially when it comes to being around people you just met, and Girl, that's how I felt after Betty lured me into the devil's web. After that day, the Lord moved on my heart and told me to give Clyde another chance.

That weekend I moved back in with him. Things were fine with us for a while until Clyde lost control of his drinking, once again. But the thing is, if he didn't get some kind of help or counseling to help him deal with his grief over losing his mother at an early age, then I was afraid he'd never get his drinking under control. He had a lot to work out with his past pain.

Girl, he eventually became verbally abusive towards me, and I wasn't going to stand for that. I told him I felt that life had more for me to explore and experience. I wasn't going to stay if he was going to abuse me.

Clyde said, "I know you want to move to Minnesota to be with your aunt and to see what life has to offer you. If you want to leave again, will you at least let my daughter stay here until you get settled? Would you consider it? Then you can come back to get her. That will give me a good amount of time to spend with my daughter; I would keep our son too, but he is still a baby, and he needs his mother." Girl, of course, I agreed because he is their father, and I wanted him to spend time with them before I left. Our son was a baby still, and he should be with me while he is a baby.

Three weeks after I arrived in Minnesota, I found a job at a family restaurant as a waitress. Thank God for my aunt, because she took care of my son until I got off from work. After about a month, I found a one-bedroom place for us.

Leaving Carbondale was the best thing for me. I met people in my new community that helped me land another job in the hotel industry, first as a hostess and then as a waitress, which helped me earn more money.

Girl, I felt so free and so alive being in a new place. I started thinking about a career as a model or even becoming an actress. For the first time, it felt good to start dreaming again. Anything is possible, right? Let's just say Minnesota was way bigger than Carbondale.

Girl, this is how you can tell when you live in a small town—everyone knows your business, which meant as a teenager, you couldn't get away with anything without the whole town knowing about it the next day. When people found out the things that happened to me in my young life, I felt invaded, and I knew it was time to relocate.

One day something happened that I found hard to believe! In my new town, I ran into someone from home. Victor lived in Carbondale, where I grew up; his family knew my family. Victor went into the Army, which is why I hadn't seen him for a while. One day I saw him, and we got together in the twin cities of Minnesota.

We stayed together for about a year before I discovered he had a bad temper, which led to physical abuse toward me and my son Derrick who was about eight months at the time. Girl, one day, I was off work, and that morning while I changed my son's diaper, I noticed he had bruises on his butt. I lost it at that moment; I went into the bedroom and asked Victor, "What happened to my son? I noticed he has bruises on his butt. Please tell me that you did not beat my son. Is that where these bruises came from?"

All he could do was stand there looking at me as if he'd done nothing wrong. I asked him again, "Why does my son have bruises on his ass, Victor? Answer me right now!" Growing up with an abusive stepdad, I snapped at that second. I was no longer afraid of him. Flashbacks of my childhood came rushing through my head. The next thing I knew, I grabbed a knife out of the drawer.

I went back to the bedroom and said, "Victor, this is the last time you will put your hands on me and my son again, you mother fucker," and I hit him in the face with my fist.

Then he came at me, fists flying, and the knife fell out of my hands. He began choking me, and I grabbed his balls with my hands until he let me go. I scrambled to pick up the knife, and I cut him on his right arm then yelled, "We're done! I want you out of here now!"

As he walked out the door, he kept saying, "Look, I'm sorry. I was angry at my boss for firing me, and when Derrick started crying and wouldn't stop, I grabbed him and began spanking him on his butt with my hand."

Girl, at that point, my adrenaline was pumping so fast, and all I could say after he finished telling me what he did to my son was, "Why, you get the hell out of my apartment and don't you ever come back here again because we are finished!"

He turned and walked away from my door, and I locked it behind him. After about fifteen to twenty minutes, he came back to the house. I was standing in the kitchen when I heard the door open. I stood next to the stove with a pot of hot boiling water, getting ready to cook dinner for me and my son.

To my surprise, he threw a stick at me. It hit the pot, and boiling water splashed on my left arm, but all I could hear was him saying, "Bitch, I'm going to kill you if I can't have you, nobody else will."

Oh, my God, even though I was in pain, I grabbed the bigger knife from my counter and went toward him with it. I tried to stab him as hard as I could, and, Girl, after I did, he just stood there as if I didn't stab him. I saw blood coming from his chest, and right at that moment, he realized I stabbed him in his chest then he ran out of my apartment.

I ran behind him, yelling, "I want my extra keys from you right now, Victor," and I saw him throw the keys at me.

After he left, I went to my neighbor's across the hall to see if she would watch my son while I went to the hospital. I knocked on her door, and she said, "Who is it?"

"Connie, your neighbor." She opened the door, and after I explained to her what happened, she said, "Girl, what the hell is wrong with these men thinking they can just take their anger out on a small child? But good for you that you stood up for yourself. I got you. Go and get that burn looked at. It could be third-degree. I'll be here when you get back from the hospital, Girl."

When I got to the hospital, it turned out it was a third-degree burn. They treated me, and after they finished, the nurse asked me what happened. I told her what my boyfriend did to my son, and that I lost it on him. Then when I put him out, he came back and did this to me.

"You should go and press charges against him," she said. "You will need a copy of the hospital papers to show the police."

I went to the police station the next day on my lunch break, and they asked me to explain what happened. I told my story about Victor's violent temper and physical abuse toward me and my son. When I finished at the police station, I got the restraining order against him, and I went back to work.

On my way home, I picked up my son, and it felt good to be home safe without feeling scared or walking on eggshells. After dinner, I relaxed on the couch with my son for a while, then I placed him in his bed and took some pain medication to ease my painful arm.

The next morning I woke up and called my boss to take the day off because I was not fit to be working that day. He gave me an okay and told me to feel better soon. I went to check the mail, and I saw Victor lying in the hallway like those drunks who have had too much and fall down on the street in doorways.

When he saw me standing there, he started begging me to give him another chance. I said to him, "Look, Victor, you and I are not getting back together. Get that out of your head. I have a restraining order on you, which means you can't be here, or you will be arrested. I'm sure you're sorry, but I can't be with a man who is violent toward my son and me."

"I know. I had no right to put my hands on you or your son, and I know now that I need to get some help for my anger. I just wanted you to know that I'm sorry before I leave."

"Well, that's great to hear, Victor, so are you going back to Carbondale?"

"I'm going back into the Army. They will help me get a counselor to deal with my anger. I know that I let my jealousy get out of control with you. I've never been with a beautiful woman like you before, and I thought if I could control you, then you wouldn't leave me for another man."

Girl, I said, "Look, if you are this jealous over me, then it only shows me that you are a weak man. I can't allow someone like this around me or my son, Victor. I think you are doing the right thing by leaving; I wish you the best." After that day, he did go back into the Army, and he got the help he needed. That was the last time I saw him.

After about a year passes by, I found a two-bedroom apartment for all of us, I went back to Carbondale to pick up my daughter, and of course, I had to see everybody before I left. After picking up my daughter, I stopped by my mom's for a visit. I also visited my grandparents.

Straight away, they said to me, "Honey, are you eating up there in the big city? You look so skinny. We know it's expensive living there in the city, and if you need to come back home, you know you are welcome at any time, okay?"

I said, "Yes, Grandma. I'm eating just fine there in the Twin Cities. I've been working a lot these days is all. I'm okay."

"If you need anything, let us know, Baby, okay?"

"Yes, I will, Grandma. I love you guys."

Once I got back to Minnesota, I went back to work, and my aunt watched the kids for me. As things started getting better for me financially, I found a great daycare for the kids.

Five years go by in Minnesota. The kids were getting older and finally began going to school. I started taking a few acting classes and performed in my first play at Theater in the Round uptown Minneapolis area. I had so much fun acting in the theater; it is in my blood, that is for sure.

Clyde repeatedly called to talk to the kids before they went to bed; I was happy to see that he was a responsible father. God knows it really helps when trying to raise two kids as a single mom.

I knew that I could make it in Minnesota on my own, but I was getting lonely, and at the same time, I wasn't ready to start dating again with all the worry of wondering if the guy I met would be normal or crazy.

Girl, it isn't easy as a single mom, especially when you try to keep your children safe and away from evil. As the years went by, the kids started asking if they could go see their dad.

You know when you look into your kids' cute beautiful brown eyes, they get to your soft spot, and unexpected thoughts come? I began thinking to myself, "Well, I haven't seen Clyde in quite a while now; maybe he's gotten stronger or even gotten some help with his drinking."

One weekend I gave him a call. He asked how the kids were doing, and I told him they were doing fine.

He said, "I live in Houston now, and things have been going very well here for me, and I was wondering if you wanted to come here to visit. I'm hoping you say yes because I would love to see the kids."

I answered, "Well, the kids have been asking to see you, and I think maybe that wouldn't be a bad idea. I guess it wouldn't hurt to come and visit for a while. I need to see if I have any vacation time coming up first before saying anything to the kids. Is that alright?"

"Sure, that's fine. Just let me know when you find out if you have any vacation time coming up, and I'll pay for your trip."

"Well, it's been killing me to ask you this question," I say.

"Well, shoot, ask me your question then."

"How's your drinking been these past four years?"

"Since I've been working with the fire department, I haven't had the time to drink that much because of the tough training that we have to do. Plus, because of the different shifts that I've been working, it's been keeping me very busy. And to be honest with you, it's just been crazy working with the fires around here in the big city. So I haven't done much drinking lately."

"I'm happy to hear that. Good for you. I'm only asking out of concern because I do care about you as my children's father. I wouldn't want them to lose their father from alcohol poisoning."

After I finished talking with Clyde, the kids and I ate dinner, and we got ready for bed. When I got to work the next day, I saw I had one week of vacation time available. Girl, the thing is, I was not really ready to go through the trouble with Clyde again. I didn't believe I had the energy to handle it. At the same time, you know that old saying, "God doesn't give us more than we can bear."

I booked a flight for us, and we headed to Houston. When we got there, Clyde was happy to see everyone. We stayed for a week, and things went fine; the kids were so happy. On our last night in Houston, Clyde began asking if we could give living together another chance, and I told him I didn't think it was a great idea for us to get back together.

He replied, "I do get what you're saying, but see you should do what's best for the kids, though, right? How about this. If I agree to go to church with you on occasion, will you give it some thought?"

"Only if you keep your word. I truly believe that if you let go of the pain from losing your mother at an early age, it would make a whole lot of difference in your life."

Once we returned to Minnesota, I gave more thought to giving Clyde another chance, but, Girl, I was leaning more toward not doing it, mainly because I was done watching him kill himself slowly.

Yet, at the same time, I wanted the kids to have that experience of having their father around as they grew up. Eventually, I decided that as long as he was willing to try, then I should at least give him another chance. I couldn't allow my doubts to deny this opportunity for the kids to be with their father.

A month later, I decided to move to Houston. I believe the lesson here was patience and trust, which I knew would be a challenge for me because of my past experiences with men. I also knew the only way I could do this again is by trusting in the Lord and staying in prayer to help me be patient with Clyde.

10: FIGHTING TEMPTATION

Girl, within a month, Clyde started telling me—not asking me—to have another child with him. He said, "I think we should have another child to clean your soul. This will get rid of the bad spirit of other men, being inside you."

"Oh, my God," I thought to myself, "What kind of bullshit is he trying to pull here?" I'd never heard anything like this coming out of Clyde's mouth or a scripture from the Bible stating this is true. Having a baby can clean your soul from the bad spirit of being with other men? What bullshit. Is this what men say to get their way?

Girl, please tell me if this doesn't sound like some made-up mess from a man who hasn't been inside a church since he was a young child.

Of course, I called him on it by saying, "Clyde, you know that's not true, right? If you want me to have another child, just ask, but please stop trying to manipulate me by using God's words against me. And certainly, don't play with my intelligence Clyde."

"Okay, you got me. I'm sorry for trying to play on your intelligence, but it's what I heard growing up. That's why I said it. But, yes, I do want another child by you. I know our children will be beautiful, like their mother."

"Not now, because I want to get into modeling and acting. Having another baby right now will cause me to put it on hold, and I'm not ready to do that, Clyde."

He just looked at me as if I was forcing him to go against his will of wanting more children. Finally, he said, "Okay, if you want to go after your career before you give it some thought, then if that's what it takes to get you to give me another child, then I will start going to AA meetings, and I will even go to see a counselor. I'm sure the fire department insurance has a list of counselors that I can choose from. Whatever it takes, I want to make you happy."

"That's great, but I don't want you to do this for me; I need you to do this for you because you want to, and that will make me happy."

Months passed, and things were going very well. I saw hope because Clyde was getting healthier and wanted more out of life. And, of course, I got pregnant with our second son Camaron.

Girl, I will say this much, I was feeling good about things between us. He was truly trying to stick with the AA meetings and seeing a counselor. He really was doing well and drinking less than his usual; he was even more tolerable to be around. However, as time passed and our youngest son was a few months old, Clyde began to slip back into his old ways of drinking early during the day and throughout the rest of the evening.

On his days off, I tried to plan things for us to do together, but the first thing he'd do when he got home from work was pour himself a drink, which meant our plans were not going to happen. I'd take the kids to the park just to get away from the house.

When we'd get back to the house, he'd be shit-faced, and I wasn't in the mood to put up with him when he was in that state. Let me ask you, Girl, have you ever been around someone who drains you when you're trying to talk some sense into them? They take all your energy.

It was not my job to play caretaker to a grown man who didn't want to stop drinking. I had my own issues that I had to deal with from my past abuse, Girl I prayed so hard, "God, have mercy on me because I don't think that I can take much more of this. If this is your will, then I will try to handle it, but I plead, Heavenly Father, please change this man so that I can do the right things by my children to raise them in a healthy home. Amen!"

Girl, I'd been in Houston for almost a year dealing with Clyde's drinking. It took a toll on me mentally, and I began to miss my own family. My mom moved to California, and one night I called to see how she was doing. She asked if I wanted to come to visit for a while and to give myself a break from Clyde. She was right; I needed a break from this situation.

I decided to go and visit my mom and everyone. When we got there, Mom was happy to see her grandkids, especially her new grandson Camaron. She asked how Clyde was doing, and I told her the same as usual. After being in California for a week, we went back to Houston, and Clyde continued to get worse.

I tried to be there for him, but with my history of growing up with my mom doing drugs and drinking, as well as other family members drinking, there's only so much a person can tolerate when putting up with someone who has a drinking problem.

I didn't think I could go through it with this man, and the only reason I came back was for our children. Girl, I was not a one-hundred percent sure that he would stay sober. He's made promises and broken them, but I decided to stay and deal with his drinking. Even though I did it for the kids, part of me wanted to hold on to the faith that one day he will see how it is affecting his family.

And then, he began being verbally abusive toward me. Girl, I was trying to make the best out of a bad situation. I hoped getting a job would help me save my sanity. I enrolled in a model and acting classes downtown Houston. I started attending right away because it helped me redirect the energy I spent thinking about Clyde's drinking. Rather than fight it, I started accepting the fact that I was stuck with this man because he's my kids' father. I wanted to channel my energy toward something that makes me happy.

So, I turned my focus on myself and my career as a model and actor. I found myself busy with dropping the kids off at school and taking our younger son to our neighbor who babysat him while I went to work. After picking up the kids from school and the neighbor, I'd fix dinner, and on the few evenings that I had classes, my neighbor looked after the kids for me until I got home.

Then things started going bad in our neighborhood. People's homes were being broken into and robbed at gunpoint. We decided it wasn't safe for us and the kids because Clyde's fire department schedule required him to work twenty-four-hours on at a time, followed by twenty-four-hours off. We thought it would be best if we moved, and we began looking for another place to live.

During his time in Houston, Clyde became friends with a couple named Brenda and Fred. They welcomed us into their home until we found a place of our own. Clyde saw this as an opportunity to save money so that we could buy a house in a nice area in Houston. I agreed that it was a great idea.

Now, Girl, I didn't know this couple like Clyde did, so this was going to be a challenge for me, and here's where I believe God was testing my strength and taking me through a life lesson. Little did I know that living with Brenda and Fred was only going to make things worse for us.

As we drove up to their house, Brenda and Fred came out on their porch to welcome us into their home. I felt a warm, kind spirit coming from Brenda. I believe God does place people in our path for a reason. After about thirty days of living in their home, I started seeing who wore the pants in that house.

Honestly, I couldn't see any way to survive this living arrangement but through my faith in God. According to the Book of Matthew chapter 26:41 NIV: "Watch and pray so that you will not fall into temptation, the spirit is willing, but the flesh is weak."

Fred was always at home whenever Brenda went to work in the morning. I'd go out to drop off the kids at school and come back to the house, but Fred was always gone when I got back. I found out later he went to his friend's house to get high.

Because we moved from our old neighborhood, I quit my job at the restaurant and canceled my evening classes because I didn't feel safe leaving my kids with Brenda and Fred. Brenda needed to be at work in the mornings and didn't have time in the evening to watch the kids.

Once again, I put my life on hold, but for a good reason, this time, especially after I checked around and saw my part-time job wouldn't cover the cost of daycare in the evening while I continue my modeling & acting classes. Girl, you wouldn't believe how much daycare cost in Houston! Oh, my God, it's ridiculous! I guessed once we got our own place again, I could start my classes again.

When Brenda walked into the house from working all day, she went straight to the kitchen and poured herself a glass of white wine. Of course, I was in the kitchen cooking dinner for everyone.

She said to me, "Have a glass of wine with me. I don't want to drink alone here, girl. I'm surprised you haven't had one already; it's a job being a mother. Girl" She started to laugh, and I grabbed a glass and poured some wine for myself.

I asked, "How was work today?"

"As usual, work is just work. It's tough dealing with insurance investigation, especially when you're trying to prove insurance fraud, Girl." She then changed topics and started talking about how she and Fred had been going through couples counseling because of his addiction to crack cocaine.

"Oh, girl, I'm deeply sorry to hear that, and I also know it's not easy dealing with it."

"It's been a battle for quite some time now, and I told him that if he continues to use, I'm gone."

"When was the last time he used?"

"It's been thirty days so far, and I'm hoping and praying that he sticks with it because I do love him. I keep telling him that he needs to change who he's hanging around, and that could make a huge difference when you're trying to fight the addiction.

So, when Freddy told me that his friend Clyde needed a place to stay, I thought to myself this could be the thing that Freddy needs to change and get his shit together. I was so happy when I met you. I saw how happy guys are, and you are a great person Connie. I see how good you are with your kids, and I like that. I'll never have that experience with children. Freddy and I had been trying; it just won't happen for me."

"Well, maybe Fred will get his act together, and you two can try again. Maybe this time, you will become a mother. Giving birth is a beautiful feeling and a great experience as a woman; it's an amazing feeling of joy. You know it's been proven that stress can cause problems with conceiving. As I said, Fred might surprise you and do a full turn around on you, and you may also be right, as this might be exactly what Clyde needs too."

"Well, if Freddy sees Clyde going to work every other day, that just might work, but I still have this doubt going on inside me. Until he gives me something to hope for, I have a hard time believing in him."

Girl, three weeks into the thirty days of living with them, Brenda got home from work and asked if I wanted to go to the grocery store with her. I said sure, but first, I wanted to let Clyde know that I was leaving so he could keep an eye on the kids. When I walked back to the bedroom, I saw Clyde sitting there with a beer in his hands, talking to Fred.

I asked, "Hey, Clyde, can I speak to you for a minute?"

"Okay, what's up?"

"Brenda told me that Fred has a bad drug addiction to crack, and I wanted to make sure you knew this in case he asked you to take him to pick up some or tries to borrow some money from you. I also want to say, look, you know we have our own issues with bad habits, now don't we? All I am saying is we don't need to add drug addiction to our current problems in our lives, especially when I have been very patient with you so far."

"Woman, what are you talking about? Bad habits?"

"You know I'm talking about your drinking, Clyde."

"Woman, please. I can't just stop whenever I want to; it's going to take some serious help from a clinical treatment center in order for me to stop drinking."

"Please promise me that you won't get maneuvered into Fred's addiction."

Clyde answered, "Okay. I got this. you don't have to worry about me; I'm stronger than you give me credit for."

Girl, when Brenda and I got back from the store, the kids were watching a movie, and my oldest daughter came up to ask me for some popcorn. So I set the groceries on the counter and put a bag in the microwave for her to share with her brother. Brenda started putting the food away in the cabinets, and I took the popcorn out of the microwave and poured it into a bowl for the kids, then went back to help Brenda put the rest of the groceries away.

When we finished, I decided to go back to see if Clyde needed anything. As I approached the bedroom, I noticed that the door was closed, and when I opened it, I saw Clyde sitting there as if he had taken a hit from the crack pipe.

Girl, I didn't want to think the worst, but because of my experience with my mother and other family members, I can tell when someone has taken a hit from a pipe. The first thing I noticed was the sweat on Clyde's nose. As soon as he looked at me, he knew that I knew.

Of course, he started walking toward me with this—oh shit, she's going to get on my ass—look on his face. Right away, I said to Clyde, "What the hell? So what happened to, 'I got this, Woman,' bullshit?"

"Woman, I *do* got this. Will you please give me a little credit? Just because I tried it doesn't mean I'm addicted to crack."

At that moment, all I could do was shake my head and walk away after saying, "Richard Pryor talked about his life of smoking crack. And look at how it took his soul. Yeah, good luck with thinking you got this."

After walking back to the kitchen, Brenda said, "What the hell, I guess we both have a man with issues. I can't believe Clyde got trapped in Freddy's mess. I figured he would be the strong one. It's not your fault that he couldn't tell Fred no; he's a grown man. It was his choice not to say yes. If it makes you feel any better, Connie, I won't give Freddy any money when I get my paycheck on Fridays."

I said, "Hell, I don't think that is going to matter at this point, Brenda. Now that he gave Clyde a taste of crack, he knows Clyde will be hooked." Brenda and I had dinner with the kids, then I put the kids to bed and read them a story. I went to watch a movie with Brenda because Fred and Clyde were still in the back-smoking crack. After the movie was over, we went to bed. At this point, I felt no reason to try anymore.

The next day when Brenda came home, she started in, "So, Freddy, please tell me that you've found a job. Is that where you're coming from right now?"

Girl, this was Brenda's life being with Fred. I understood what she was going through as I was also going through it with Clyde.

I continued to stay on Clyde, trying to keep him straight, because I did not want to end up worse off than Brenda. Not too long later, we found a place of our own to purchase and began the buying process. Soon Brenda could have her own space back.

Girl, you know what it's like to have people live with you but not show appreciation? That is why I always cleaned up after my family. When Brenda came home, she'd find a good smelling house with great vibration and dinner cooking.

When Clyde came home from the fire station the next morning, it was like Fred couldn't wait for him to walk through the door. I was on my way out to drop the kids off at school, and when I returned, Fred was out back with Clyde in the garage playing pool and talking.

I yelled out to Clyde, "Hey, can I talk to you for a second?"

"Sure, Baby, I'll be right there; give me a minute. I'm about to kick Fred's ass on this pool table."

I stood there in the kitchen, making breakfast for Camaron and me, and I poured a cup of coffee for myself. Then I sat at the breakfast table and began feeding Camaron while I waited for Clyde to come inside. Eventually, Clyde walks into the kitchen, asking, "What's up, Baby?"

I said, "You tell me what's up. Fred isn't around when you're not here, but as soon as you come home, he can't wait to hang out. I'm asking you, do I have to worry about you because you are the major breadwinner in this family? If you lose it, then you put our family at risk. That's all I'm saying, Clyde. I'm asking you, is there something I need to be aware of?"

"Look, I'm here with my family, aren't I?"

"And your point is? In case you aren't aware, smoking crack costs money. That's my point here. Your being here with your family is not my issue in case you were wondering."

"Fred hasn't asked me for anything. I'm hoping that he doesn't, because I saw how mad Brenda can get, and I don't want no part of that."

"Well, that's good to hear. I hope you'll be strong because it's our family that I'm concerned about, not Fred. I just wanted you to be aware of how I feel about him involving you in his crack addiction in the first place."

After I finished feeding our son, I put him in his playpen and finished my breakfast. Once I was done, I took out something to cook for dinner. Then I headed out back to ask Clyde if he'd put the down payment on the house and did he have any new news about it, and I asked if he could go and pick the kids up from school.

"Sure, I can pick up the kids for you, and far as the house goes, we are in the process of signing everything. I'll keep you posted, okay? Do I have to go right now? What time is it?"

I answered, "Yes, you do. You guys have been out here playing pool for a while now."

After he got back with the kids, Clyde says to me, "Fred wants me to take him to the store."

Girl, I raised my left eyebrow at him, and I said, "Sure, Clyde, I'll see you later then."

"You know that you can count on me. I learned my lesson, and I know when to throw in the towel when it comes to angering you, Baby. I know not to let this come between me and my family, right?"

"Oh, really? Well, you do know how to butter a woman up for sure, and it all sounds great."

When Brenda got home from work, she asked me, "Has Freddy been here? I told him that if he doesn't find a job soon, he may as well pack his stuff and get out."

"Well, I'm not sure if he's been out looking for work unless he went this morning. He was up when Clyde came in this morning, but I'm not one-hundred percent sure what he did after that. What I do know he and Clyde played pool out back since noon, and then Clyde went to pick up the kids for me. After he got back home, Fred asked Clyde to take him to the store."

Brenda responded, "girl, I know what kind of store, alright. I'm not fucking around with Freddy; he's not taking me seriously, and I guess I need to really show Freddy that I'm not playing with him. As soon as he gets back here, I got something for his ass, and now he's dragging Clyde into his mess."

So Brenda and I sat at the dining room table, having a glass of wine while the kids ate their dinner. Of course, Clyde and Fred still hadn't made it home from the so-called store. Girl, tell me, why do men play games? Because now Clyde is starting to lie to me, and that is not good for our relationship as parents.

Eventually, we saw headlights pulling up to the front of the house. It was them, and as soon as they walked into the house, I said, "Clyde, so is this what we have become now? You lying to me? Because if so, I'm done, and I'm out of here."

I walked out of the living room and into the back bedroom. I heard Brenda yelling at Fred. She began taking his clothes out of her dresser drawers in their bedroom and threw them down the hallway, yelling, "Fred, get your shit and get out of my house! I'm so done with you!"

Then Clyde comes walking into our bedroom, saying, "Look, woman, I didn't lie to you. Fred had me take him to the house of one of his friends. When I saw that he was in there too long, I went in and got him. That's when we came home. Now I don't believe he was in there smoking crack; I saw him get some marijuana, though.

Now, what is wrong with that, Baby? I think you are being way too hard on me. I know we are here to save money to get our own place. Fuck, Woman, give me some credit. That's all I ask, will you give me that please? Now look, Brenda's kicking Fred out of the house."

"I'll go talk with her and try and calm her down. No, there's nothing wrong with weed, but I can see where Brenda is coming from. Fred needs to show her that he cares enough to get out there and find a job, then maybe she will relax a little."

I walked into Brenda's room, "Hey, girl, you need to calm down. Now Clyde told me that Fred didn't buy any crack; it was only weed. Weed isn't bad; it's for anxiety and stress, and judging right now, it wouldn't hurt if you smoked a little and girl, I'm afraid you are going to give yourself a heart attack. Let's go out on the deck and chill for a minute."

"Yeah, you're right. I'm about to give myself a stroke around here, girl. I'm so tired of dealing with Freddy about his addiction problem. I want him to give a damn; that is all." As we both relaxed out back, the guys started playing a game of pool. Brenda and I finally went to bed because we both had to get up the next morning, and I had to get the kids off to school.

11: BLESSING THE HOUSE

A few weeks later, we finally got the paperwork back for the townhouse we chose to buy; it was in a very nice neighborhood. One day, after getting settled into our home, I walked to the mailbox and noticed a car driving slowly, and when I turned to walk toward my house, a guy rolled down his window. He asked, "Do you know where Clyde lives?" Girl, of course I knew, but I wasn't going to tell him that I did.

I told him I didn't know where Clyde lived. Clearly, he didn't know what Clyde's woman looked like, because he accepted my answer. The driver didn't know where Clyde lived, and I want it to stay that way. However, I saw he was still watching me, so I started walking very slowly back to the row of houses so that he wouldn't see which townhouse I went into. Once I noticed that he pulled out of our community, I walked up to our door and opened it.

Clyde was coming out as I was coming in; I asked him, "Did you tell a dope dealer where we live?"

"Why?"

"Well, because I just got stopped by some guy in a new black Cadillac with tinted windows asking if I knew where Clyde lived."

"Baby, I never told anyone where we lived. It must have been Fred who I told this guy. Fred owes me money, so I told him where we live, but I'll give him a call and tell him not to tell the dope man what townhouse I live in."

Girl, don't you know that as soon as he spoke with Fred, the next thing I knew, a few days later, this dope dealer came back over to the townhouse.

Keep in mind once we had gotten all settled into our place, I started going to church. One Sunday after service, I asked the pastor if he would come out to my house and bless it with some holy oil, or could he give me some so I could do the blessing myself.

I needed to keep my house safe from evil people, and of course, the pastor said, "Sister Connie, if you are having a problem with someone in your neighborhood, maybe you should call the police."

"No, Pastor, it's just people with bad spirits that I am worried about. I only want to bless my house with the oil to ward off the evil spirits, and to keep them from entering my home is all."

Girl, once he blessed the oil, he gave it to me. After service that Sunday, I took the holy oil home and started saying a prayer, "Heavenly Father, I pray that you would protect me and my family from all the evil and from those that would seek to harm us. Uphold us and keep us safe from all the evil that encircle our lives. Put your hedge of protection and safety around us; we pray and place a guard at our doors and protect us from all that pass by our gate.

And, Father, keep our hearts from fear but rather fill us to overflowing with your peace that passes all understanding. Thank you that you are indeed our refuge and strength. You are that ever-present help in time of trouble. In your strength, we will not fear, though the earth be removed, and though the mountains be carried into the middle of the sea. Stay with us wherever we go. In Jesus's name, Amen."

Unfortunately, the drug dealer was determined to find where Clyde lived and eventually found the right door to knock on.

Clyde went to the door, opened it, and said, "Man, how did you find out where I live? I never told you."

Girl, of course, Clyde walked out to talk to him. A few minutes later, Clyde and the dealer came back inside through the kitchen, and Clyde offered him a seat at the dining room table! Girl, do you know what that man said to me after sitting there for ten minutes?

He said, "It is awfully hot in here; just tell Clyde that I'll wait for him outside."

I told him that was fine, and I'd let Clyde know. Clyde came back downstairs, and he asked me where Tony went.

I replied, "He said that it was too hot in here, so he told me to tell you that he'll wait for you outside."

Girl, Tony felt the heat from the prayer I put on our house with the holy oil that I got from church the previous Sunday.

When Clyde walked back into the house, he asked, "What happened? That man ran out of here scared, and all he said to me was, 'Clyde if you need anything, you just call me because I'm not coming back into your house again. I've never felt so uncomfortable from being in someone's home. I got so hot I felt like I was on fire. Man, it's a hundred degrees outside, don't your air conditioner work?'" Clyde continued to tell me what happened, "I told him, 'Man, my house feels great, and yes, our air conditioning does work, and it is on.' Look, I don't know why he would say that when it feels cold in here right now."

That's when I said to Clyde, "I had the pastor pray over some holy oil on Sunday; he said I prayed over the oil for you to use. When I came home, I said a prayer and placed the holy oil all over the house, especially over the back and front door. This holy oil will keep out the evil that crosses our doorstep."

Girl, when you stand in faith, and you believe, God's most powerful archangels will protect you. I honestly believed it was one of God's angels who had turned up the heat under this guy's seat so he would leave our house.

And oh mine, it worked! I was so happy to see that God answered our prayers when I needed his help to protect us from evil.

Girl, after I told Clyde about the holy oil, he said, "Honey, whatever you did, it truly scared him to the point that he had sweat falling off his face, even when our air conditioning is on full blast. Then that dealer said to me, 'Clyde, are you telling me that you are done smoking? I tell you what, how about if you sell it, and in turn, you can enjoy it as well. One thing I notice about you, Clyde, you got your shit together, man. Just let me know if you change your mind, and when you do, I'll meet you outside your place.'"

Then I said to Clyde, "Praise God for his protection."

However, even though the holy oil got the dealer out of our house, he must have given Clyde something that day, because not too long after the dealer was gone, Clyde's co-worker Mike knocked on the door.

Clyde answered the door, and the two of them went upstairs to the bedroom. I wondered why Mike was coming over more than usual on the days that they both were off. Eventually, I realized Mike came over to hang out with Clyde, and they would start drinking then end up in our bedroom smoking crack. After getting high, the two of them came down to the living room to play a game of pool.

Girl, I was tired of talking and arguing with Clyde about his drinking and doing drugs, and I didn't know what else I could do at this point. One day my neighbor Melanie says to me, "girl, you have to think about yourself and the kids at this point. I have a cousin that is on that stuff too, and it gets worse before it gets better."

One of the things I did to stay sane was reenroll in evening courses, which happened on the nights Clyde was off work. At that time, we had only one vehicle, a Chevy van, and I'd drive to class in the evenings while Clyde watched the kids.

One evening I'm getting ready to head to class, and Clyde, just to get under my skin, takes off with the van and rides around with the kids. He knew how dangerous it was for me to take the bus to class.

So Girl, that evening, I stood at the bus stop, and my college instructor happened to drive by. He stopped and asked, "Connie, would you like a ride because it's not safe for you to be standing out here by yourself."

Of course, I said yes because not too long before, a few women came up missing or were murdered in the Houston downtown area. Ed told me about that once we began driving.

He asked me, "Why are you taking the bus to get to class? Is everything alright at home?"

I said, "Yes, it is. My kids' dad doesn't think I should want a career other than to be a mother to his children. That is why he took off with the van this evening."

Ed said, "You are so beautiful and smart. Well, some men can't handle a beautiful woman, and it's kind of sad for him because forcing a woman to do something against her will may eventually cause a man to lose the woman. I was always taught to support your wife and her dreams and goals. You will have a peaceful and joyful life at some point. I know it."

After thanking him for the ride to my house, we said good night to each other.

Once I got home, I went straight to our bedroom, where Clyde sat on the bed watching TV with a drink on the nightstand as if he did nothing wrong.

Girl, I was so mad at him taking off with the van that evening, and clearly, he knew what he was doing. All he could say was, "I know what I agreed to, and in my opinion, I think it's a waste of your time to go back to school when you need to think about being a mother to our kids, why do you need work when I make enough to take care of us. Your focus should be on helping our kids with their homework, not worrying about yourself at this point."

Wow! Girl, can you believe this shit? After he left for work, I got the older kids off to school. Our younger son, Camaron, was about a year old now, and we ate breakfast, then we went to our neighbor's house two doors down.

Her name was Martha. She was an older woman with lots of wisdom, and when I told her about wanting to make a difference with my life, she was happy for me. She thought it was a great idea for me to want something more out of life as a woman than just being a stay at home mother.

She said, "We women need to always be independent for ourselves. Out here in the world, a woman should never fully rely on a man. That way, you will never be left out in the cold or disappointed."

Girl, she even offered to watch my son for me if I wanted to continue my classes. I was so happy to hear that!

12: AN UNEXPECTED SURPRISE

For a while, everything was going well. Then a few months later, I found out I was pregnant. I was on the pill, so how the hell did that happen? I told myself, this baby isn't going to happen; we didn't need any more kids.

At that point, I was still dealing with Clyde and his drinking and possible crack addiction; it wasn't a great idea to have more children by him.

When I told him I was pregnant, and that wasn't a great idea to bring another baby into our lives, he got mad, walked out of the house, and slammed the door behind him. Eventually, when he came back to the house, of course, he tried to talk me into keeping the baby. I told him I just wasn't ready to have another child right then.

He responded, "If that's how you feel, then I'll give you the money to get rid of it when I get paid next week."

Well, Girl, that payday never came, and months went by, and I ended up going through with the pregnancy.

Meanwhile, I stopped working at the restaurant and got a job doing hair for a friend of Melanie's. One day, as I was working, I went into premature labor. I was halfway finishing with a customer's hairstyle, and I decided to call my doctor's office. His assistant told me she would give my doctor the message. Soon after my call, I heard my phone ring.

I answered it, "Hello?"

It was the doctor, "Hi, Connie, I can't believe that you're going into labor. You're only thirty-two weeks along. How far apart are your labor pains? Have you been keeping track of them?"

"They are forty-five to fifty minutes apart right now."

AN UNEXPECTED SURPRISE

"Well, if you are right in the middle of doing hair, which my assistant told me, I guess you can take a few shots of whiskey, and that will give you enough time to finish with your customer. But if your labor pains get to twenty minutes apart, you need to come to the hospital right away."

Girl, as I finished with my customer's hair, my labor pains started to come every fifteen minutes. Oh, my God, I was pushing it very close. My neighbor drove me to the hospital, and while on the way, he called Clyde to let him know that I was going into labor, and we were on our way to the hospital.

Once we got to the hospital, the doctor came into my hospital room and said, "Okay, let's get you ready to deliver these triplets."

"Look, Doc, now isn't the time for jokes. These labor pains are kicking my ass right now. Can you give me an epidural to take away the pain?"

Girl, this baby was coming, and I started pushing. Then the doctor said to me, "From the looks of it, you won't need an epidural. At this point, the baby is already coming; I can see the crown of the baby's head. You're doing very well, Connie. Keep pushing; it's coming. That's it." After the last push, he said to me, "It's a girl."

He began pressing on my stomach to help expel the placenta, and as he reached forward to cut my new baby's umbilical cord, he said, "Oh mine; I'm not joking now, Connie. It's another baby. But she's coming out by her feet, so I have to turn her around."

Girl, by the way, this doctor had huge hands, which he was about to put inside me to turn the baby around. And let me tell you, it hurt like hell while he was doing it. After he finished, he said, "You have another girl, and they are fraternal twins, meaning one egg split into two. What are you going to name them?"

"Two of them?" I was still in shock from what just happened, and he's asking me what I'm going to name them?

"Oh my, how did I miss the second heartbeat when you came in for your last ultrasound?"

"Sorry, Doc, I can't help you with that question other than saying God had a plan for her."

After giving birth to twin girls, I was exhausted, but at the same time elated. I said, "Dr. Johnson, I would like my tubes tied right now."

"Are you sure about this? You're still young. Shouldn't you talk this over with your husband before making this decision?"

"First of all, we're not married. Secondly, this isn't his body; it's mine, and I'm telling you that this is what I want before I leave this hospital."

"Okay, if that's what you want, I'll do it."

"Yes! It's what I want." I wasn't about to be stuck with more babies by Clyde. Hell no! At that point, I didn't believe Clyde would ever stop drinking.

As it turns out, while I was in the hospital, he had one of his co-workers over to the house, and apparently, they had been smoking crack upstairs in our bedroom. I figured I didn't need to suffer alongside him. Clyde was not going to deal with his past, and now he's added another habit to his drinking problem.

I started preparing myself to leave him. As the twins got older, I went back to work. That way, when I was ready to go back to Minnesota, I'd be better prepared.

13: FINALLY, I'M FREE

I went to visit my sister Edwina in Minnesota, and while I was there, she arranged for me to dance at a couple of private parties—topless dancing—with her, and I made some really good money. While working those parties, I was happy for the first time in a long time. I felt free-spirited.

And I do believe in my heart that's when I met my twin flame; the two of us were so free-spirited together. We really enjoyed ourselves at the party. When we first laid eyes on each other, I felt a deep sense of connection with him, and I knew that somehow our souls belonged together. However, I guess the universe had different plans for us.

At the time we met, I had things going on, and so did he. Our timing just wasn't right. The next day, I took a flight back to Houston.

When I arrived home, of course, it was the same old thing with Clyde. He didn't want anything out of life other than to work and come home and drink and do drugs. I'd been in Houston for over five years, and nothing had changed.

I could tell Clyde was getting angry that I didn't want to continue living with his life of using and drinking. I wanted to travel and see the world. I created a five-year goal and wanted to take on projects like going to another country, helping build a school for homeless young girls, or help other abused women. Girl, after watching him destroy his own life with drugs and alcohol, I wanted to live mine.

During those years, I continued with acting classes. Graduation was coming right up. For the final performing arts assignment, we each got to choose a character from a book called *For Colored Girls Who Have Considered Suicide/When The Rainbow Is Enuf*" by Ntozake Shange.

Who would have thought this would be the book that Ms. King, our acting instructor, would choose for the class to perform on graduation night. I guess she wanted to see how good our acting skills were before handing us graduation certificates.

And, Girl, it turned out so nice. I did well enough at the rehearsal that she gave me two characters to play that evening. We had a full house that night, and everyone was standing at the end of our performance. That's when I knew I wanted more for my life.

Ms. King planned a party for us after the show. It was nice for everyone to enjoy our last time seeing each other. We all had plans to get into theater and acting one day. When I got home, I told the kids about my performance, and they were happy to hear that everything turned out so well.

After reading them a bedtime story, I gave them a hug and kiss and said good night. Clyde was in the living room with his friend, Michael, from work, and of course, the two of them were smoking crack. I said, "Clyde, I need to talk to you, please!" He came into the kitchen, and Michael walked out the door.

I said, "You know, Clyde, I just can't be with you anymore because this isn't love to me. All this feels like is an arrangement, and it's certainly not any kind of way to raise our kids. This is not normal. You and I both know all we do is argue every other day, and it's always about your addiction. That's not healthy for me or the kids. Or, would you be happier if I smoked crack right beside you? Is this what you want? Let me answer that question for you. Hell, no! I refuse to become a crackhead like my mother."

"Why can't you love me? It's not like I don't want to support you and your dreams. I just don't want to lose you to a rich man. The more I think about it, the more I get scared."

Girl, after hearing this, I thought, "So now it's me that's keeping you from changing your bad habit? Okay, Mister Let's-sabotage-her-life-because-of-my-insecurities, I'm gonna tell you how it is."

I said to him, "Clyde, hear me. First, you knew that I didn't love you in that way. Second, the only reason I stayed with you is that I felt safe when I was younger. Now we're adults, and all we have to show for these years together are our beautiful kids."

He sat there listening, trying to make sense of everything. I followed up, "You and I don't have anything in common, nor do we want the same things in life. Why make things harder on each other? Why not allow us to leave with grace? Besides, I do believe you enjoyed the ride while it lasted, and in the process, we have five beautiful children."

"Yes, we did create five beautiful children together. I don't think we should split them up just because you don't love me. People stay together for worse reasons than that."

"So, you want our children to believe that fighting and arguing is normal? Wouldn't you want them to be in healthy relationships as adults and with someone that they truly love?"

Clyde stood there with a glassy-eyed look of disappointment on his face and said, "I'll give it some thought and get back to you on this."

Girl, then the phone rang like it was divine intervention, and Clyde answered. At that point, the only thing on his mind was getting out of the house to meet with his co-worker Michael. As soon as he ended the call, he said, "I'm leaving for a little bit. Can we pick this conversation up later?" And there he went, Girl, out the door. I just went upstairs to take a shower and go to bed.

Thank God the next day was Saturday. I was happy because I didn't have any homework to get done, and I didn't have to work the weekend. I felt good about my life and that I'd told Clyde what was on my mind about going our separate ways.

That next evening he came home after he got off shift, Michael was with him, and they started a game of pool. After pool and some drinking, they went upstairs to smoke some crack.

I found myself in the bedroom with them, and Clyde said, "Maybe if you smoke a little. It might loosen you from being so uptight all the time."

Out of anger, I said, "You know what? Okay, I'll try it. We'll see how bad things get if I become addicted as you." I took the pipe from him and hit it!

Oh, my God, Girl, it was such a rush at first, but after about twenty to thirty minutes, the high was gone. The next day I felt so ashamed for what I had done.

When I woke, I prayed to God for his forgiveness. Later that morning, Clyde came downstairs. I stood there with a cup of coffee in my hands and said, "Look, I wanted to try it. And to be completely honest with you, it wasn't all that. The high was only temporary; it's not worth spending money on. As Richard Pryor said, it's a rich man high. With that said, I'm convinced that you and I have two different ideas of doing fun stuff together. It looks like your idea of fun is getting high together."

At that point, he began verbally abusing me. I'm sorry, but I will not stay with a man who thinks just because he's providing a roof, thinks he can get away with that behavior. Let my experience be a lesson for you; crack affects people differently, and it's not for me. Girl, do not stay in a verbally or physically abusive relationship for that reason. You should stay because he treats you well, and he loves you for who you are. Stay with a man because you really love him, not because of what he can do for you. Am I right or wrong, Girl?

So, that night I said a prayer, "Dear God, please give Clyde peace, and allow him to accept the truth that our time has come to a crossroad. Help him understand it's time to let go of any false hope of being together, Amen."

In a sense, after saying the prayer, God gave me peace about my decision, and he also gave me the courage and the confidence to let go of feeling sorry for Clyde because it was hindering him from moving on.

God did not intend for us to be unhappy with a person out of pettiness, and I also do not believe God wants us to settle with someone just because he can provide material things for us.

When we trust in God, he will provide those things for us, but because of the way many of us were brought up, we stop believing in the plan God has for us.

Girl, I don't know about you, but I don't want my last days on earth to be living with someone that I don't love.

I deserve the life that God intended for me, and I will hold strong to the faith that one day I will meet the man God has in mind for me. I believe the universe will lead us together in the near future. I want to be happy and experience true love in my life.

The next day when I came downstairs, Clyde sat in the chair by the pool table, and it appeared he'd been up all night. Well, even though God had given me strength, I still held those old beliefs of being a caretaker to someone's weakness.

It did not matter whether it was drugs or alcohol or something else. As I saw him sitting there looking sad, I started to fall back into my caretaking ways.

Then I heard the voice of the Lord speaking to me. "Do not fall back to your old ways. Set yourself free, like an eagle."

At that moment, I knew I had to make arrangements to pack up my things. The kids and I had to leave. I wasn't going to wait around for Clyde to think about anything anymore.

Girl, dealing with Clyde's drinking and crack use was just too much stress. The only way a person truly is free from their past pain is by giving it over to God and allow the healing to begin. Being truthful about my life story will one day save someone's life.

I went through suffering and struggles in life, and when I came to my breaking point in my life, I surrendered to God. That's when He transformed me into the person I was meant to become.

Letting go of shame means being totally honest with yourself, and by doing so, your life begins to balance out for the greater good.

So, after Clyde got to work that day, he called me, "Hey, I have been thinking. If you want to leave and move to Minnesota, I won't stand in your way. When you get there, just give me a call and let me know that you made it there safely. I will help you with the kids; no matter what, I will always help you and the kids."

Girl, I was so thankful that God gave Clyde peace about everything, and it was music to my ears that he was going to help me with the kids.

Before this decision about moving out had been finalized, I'd been working on my career. Now I was really glad I had because it gave me potential opportunities for work after I left.

I'd created a resume to send out to the agencies that Ms. Racheal King suggested to us before graduation. I sent my resumes to about ten agencies, most of which were in Florida, California, and Georgia. I was pleased and surprised to get a response from and agency in Florida.

Girl, if you could only feel how thrilled I felt when I received a call from Timothy with John Casablanca's Modeling Girl! The timing was perfect, and I was so glad I didn't miss his call before leaving the next day.

He asked if I could send him a few body shots and another headshot. He said once he received them, he would contact me.

After Clyde got home, we sat down and talked about how we would handle shared custody. He agreed to keep our two older kids Keeonda and Derrick, until I got to Minnesota and got on my feet.

My mom moved back to Minnesota two years prior, and she only had a two-bedroom apartment. I bought the tickets for me and the kids to leave that weekend for Minnesota.

I said, "Clyde, it's only fair that you share in child support; wouldn't you agree?"

He replied, "You're right. I just thought since we are splitting them up for filing taxes, then we should share in shared custody as well."

I said, "Okay, we can do that, but when you bring the two older kids to Minnesota, I will be filing for them; does that sound fair?"

"Yes, I agree with it."

After we both decided what we were going to do, I heard the kids coming down the stairs, and we explained to them that Mommy and Daddy decided that it would be best if we didn't live together anymore because we weren't happy.

We told them that God blessed us with great kids, and we would always love them. We also assured them that once Mommy got to Minnesota and found a place big enough for everyone, Daddy would bring you two to Minnesota to live with Mommy.

Girl, I could see in their little faces that they were confused, especially Keeonda, because she was a Daddy's girl. She was so sad, but kids had an instinct to sense when something is wrong.

Our son Derrick came over to me and gave me a hug. He said, "Mommy, I will miss you but are we coming soon?"

Girl, he was a Mommy's boy. I told him, "Well, Mommy will get there and get things set up right away. I'll make sure Daddy knows that I'm ready for him to bring my sweet boy to me very soon, okay?"

He said, "Okay, Mommy. I love you."

Now my older daughter was mad at me, and she just went up to her room and closed the door. Clyde said, "I'll go up and talk to her. She's just taking this the hardest because she wants us to stay together. Plus, you know she's a Daddy's girl."

I said, "Yes, I know she is, which is why I think I should go up and talk with her instead of you."

"Okay, if you think that's best."

"Yes, I do."

I headed upstairs, and when I opened her door, she was lying on her bed reading a book. I walked over and sat right beside her, saying, "Look, Honey, I know that you want Daddy and Mommy to be together, but Mommy and Daddy are not in love like normal couples. All we do is argue and fight about his drinking and other things that you wouldn't understand right now. Sweetie, that kind of communication is not good for kids to hear every day of their lives. It just isn't healthy for you to grow up around that, Sweetheart.

If I could change how I feel, you know I would, but I can't. Someday I hope that you can understand this decision better. So far, God gave me peace about my decision, and I want you to know that I will not move to Minnesota and forget about you and your brother.

Honey, this doesn't mean that you can't come and visit your Dad after you move to Minnesota with me. Whenever you want to visit him, all you have to do is let me know. In fact, if you want to come back to Texas for the summer after school is over, I'll make sure to talk with your dad about that. How's that sound to you?"

She said, "Okay, Mommy." She gave me a hug, then said, "I love you."

The next morning the three younger children and I took a cab to the Amtrak train station, and we all arrived safely at my mom's house.

She even cooked dinner for us. After everyone had eaten, I put the kids pj's on and put them in bed. I said good night, kissed them, and said, "Mommy loves you, but I'm too tired for a story tonight. I'll make it up to you guys this week; how's that sound?"

"Okay, goodnight Mommy," they said sweetly. I went back into the living room to spend a little time with Mom before I went to bed.

The next morning I went out to search for work, and when I got back, Mom and the kids were watching television together. It was so nice to be around my family even though they were dysfunctional. I felt good being there in Minneapolis-St. Paul Minnesota.

I was so excited that I made the right choice to say goodbye to Houston, Texas; to be honest, I missed the four seasons. And, and I wasn't happy being in Texas without family. Being here in Minnesota is like the beginning of a new life for me and a fresh start.

Now, I am near my mom's brother and sister, as well as my aunt and uncle; they live in a different part of Minnesota.

Now that I'm here, it feels like home again. I am ready to experience and see what the universe has planned for me.

Girl, I'm happy about the next step on my journey of discovering God's plan for my life. I can't wait to share it with you, because you are now my best friend in the whole world.

Girl, I will see you in my next story tale book. So, until then, know that I love you. God bless you and keep you safe. Namaste!

This Anger is No Longer Mine

Made in the USA
Columbia, SC
25 October 2020